TO SEIZE THEIR LANDS

Manifest Destiny in Washington Territory

Guy Breshears

HERITAGE BOOKS
2011

HERITAGE BOOKS
AN IMPRINT OF HERITAGE BOOKS, INC.

Books, CDs, and more—Worldwide

For our listing of thousands of titles see our website
at
www.HeritageBooks.com

Published 2011 by
HERITAGE BOOKS, INC.
Publishing Division
100 Railroad Ave. #104
Westminster, Maryland 21157

Copyright © 2011 Guy Breshears

Other books by the author:
Loyal till Death: A Diary of the 13th New York Artillery
Major Granville Haller: Dismissed with Malice

Cover photograph: Final resting spot of Brigadier General George Wright, United States Army (1803–1865); Old City Cemetery; Sacramento, California. Photo by author.

All rights reserved. No part of this book may be reproduced or transmitted in any form or by any means, electronic or mechanical, including photocopying, recording or by any information storage and retrieval system without written permission from the author, except for the inclusion of brief quotations in a review.

International Standard Book Numbers
Paperbound: 978-0-7884-5305-2
Clothbound: 978-0-7884-8733-0

TABLE OF CONTENTS

1800: Ash and prophetic dreams	1
1801-1850: Origins to the Cayuse War	2
1851-1854: Setting the stage	8
1855: Treaties and War	12
1856-1857: A troubled peace	28
1858: Disaster for the tribes	34
1859-1860: A phony war	45
1861-1889: Return to Stability	50
Guide to the Sites and Personnel of the Washington Territory Indian Wars	52
Locations of battles and places by county	54
Military Timeline of Washington Territory	104
Treaty of Medicine Creek, 1854	131
Treaty of Point Elliott, 1855	137
Treaty of Point No Point, 1855	145
Treaty of Neah Bay, 1855	152
Treaty of Yakama, 1855	158
Treaty of Walla Walla, 1855	164
Treaty of Quinault, 1856	172
Preliminary articles of a treaty of peace and friendship between the United States and the Spokane nation of Indians, 1858	177
Preliminary articles of a treaty of peace and friendship between the United States and the Coeur d' Alene Indians, 1858	180
Letters: Apprehensions towards war	183

Photos of historical sites 194

Bibliography 199

INTRODUCTION

The cause of the war is, that the Americans are going to seize their lands. Living in Yakama Indian country Father Charles Pandosy, OMI wrote these words, in April, 1853, to a fellow priest about the heightened state of agitation among the Indian tribes concerning their feelings toward the Americans. Most of Father Pandosy's superiors thought he was exaggerating the threat and deemed him an alarmist. Little did anyone know that in just over two years there would be war because the Americans were going to seize their lands.

When Thomas Jefferson gave his first inaugural address, he spoke of a "rising nation, spread over a wide and fruitful land, traversing all the seas…[and] advancing rapidly beyond the reach of mortal eye." With this speech he set in motion a series of government policies to seize and defend the expanding frontiers of the United States and these collective policies would later be called Manifest Destiny.

It wasn't the Americans who first tried to obtain the land for their government; that honor most likely goes to the Spanish. They claimed the Pacific Ocean as their exclusive territory based upon the Treaty of Tordesillas of 1494. Great Britain opposed this by arguing that ocean navigation was opened to all and that any territorial claims had to be backed by occupation.

Starting with the year 1774 Spain sent several naval expeditions to the Northwest. Within a few years they had explored the mouth of the Columbia River northwards to Sitka. From these explorations Spain claimed the Northwest for their own and seized several British ships to strengthen her claims. As both sides prepared for war they also started to negotiate a series of agreements known as the Nootka Conventions which left Great Britain as the dominate power in the Pacific Northwest until challenged by the United States several years later.

During the spring of 1792 they landed near present day Neah Bay with the intentions of making it a permanent Spanish outpost in the Pacific Northwest. It didn't last long as the harbor and outpost were found to have limitations. The dreams of a Spanish Northwest Empire were abandoned by winter and they concentrated on the lands in the Pacific southwest. Any Spanish rights to the Northwest were given to the Americans by the Adams-Onís Treaty of 1819.

With the Spanish out of the way the next country to try and seize the Northwest was the British. Their method was the domination of the fur trading business in the region. In 1821 the Hudson's Bay Company had acquired its rival the Northwest Company and all of its trading posts around the area. This included the Spokane House, near present day Spokane, and Fort George, near the mouth of the Columbia River.

By 1824 the Hudson's Bay Company decided to establish a new headquarters on the north bank of the Columbia River. The reasons were many but it was generally thought that the Columbia River would be the border between British and American territories. The British founded Fort Vancouver and worked towards establishing their claims on the Northwest and keeping the Americans out.

The British effort to keep the Americans out was to be in vain. History fell upon the Americans to seize the lands from those who already lived there. This is their story.

The purpose of this book is not a complete history of the conquest of Washington Territory. Instead, I have given a starting place for those interested in the military history of the region. A guide for the student of state history who wants to explore and discover important events that happened here rather than being told nothing happened here.

It should be noted that when I list those who served in the Territory many of them are buried here. For a variety of reasons I have decided not to list where they are buried. It is up to the reader to discover where their final resting place is.

I have also included sites in both Oregon and Idaho. This was done because these sites are integral parts of the wars in the Territory and not to include them would be negligent on the part of history.

If there are any mistakes or errors in this book I alone take responsibility for them. Therefore, I would like to thank the following people for their help over the years in assisting and encouraging me: Jim Tyrrell, Joe Cravens, Annie Bailey, Dr. Martin Chamberlain, Keith and Nancy Storey, Mark Berhow, Dr. JWT Youngs, Dr. Charles Mutschler, Fr. Kevin Valliancourt, the great staff at Heritage Books and anyone else who has encouraged me or asked me questions about the wars of Washington Territory. Last but not least to Peggy Chan for being part of my life.

This book is dedicated to those that baptized the territory with their blood and especially to Our Lady of Good Help; Patroness of the State of Washington and my Mother. May I have help when I am finally called.

1800: Ash and prophetic dreams

In the summer of 1800 a new religion came alive among the Indians of the Columbia Plateau when ash fell upon them. For many of them the ash seemed liked the end of the world and this caused a change in their societal structure; from this change a religion known as the Plateau Prophets, or Dreamers, was born and it "promised to restore the human relationship with the spirit world while preparing people for the disruptive events to come."[1] The Prophets pronounced a new theology in which a supernatural being called Chief had created the world and predestined its ending.[2]

The Chief had said, "I will send messages to earth by the souls of people that reach me, but whose time to die has not yet come." [3]These people were the Prophets who all dreamed they had visited the land of the dead and had spoken directly with the Chief. After the visit the Chief commanded them to return and tell their people the messages that had been given.

One of the Prophets from the Spokane tribe, named Silimxnotylmilakobok, proclaimed, "Soon there will come from the rising sun a different kind of man from any you have yet seen, who will bring with them a book and will teach you everything, and after that the world will fall to pieces."[4]

Another Prophet spoke:

---

[1] Larry Cebula, "Religious Change and Plateau Indians: 1500-1850", 72
[2] Christopher Miller, *Prophetic Worlds,* 43-44
[3] Ibid., 44
[4] Ibid., 45

There is a vision before me now of things to come. Far to the East, I see a pale-faced people pushing the red-man back to the setting sun. The red-men fight this onward march to no avail. They are driven away from the lands of their forefather; their dead lie strewn along the trails…You are a happy people now, but you will not always remain so. For many snows the same fate will come to you. [5]

1801-1850: Origins to the Cayuse War

On March 4, 1801 Thomas Jefferson was sworn in as President of the United States and gave his inaugural address that launched the policy that would later be called Manifest Destiny, the military expansion and defense of the western frontiers. He spoke of a "rising nation, spread over a wide and fruitful land, traversing all the seas with the rich productions of their industry…[and] advancing rapidly to destinies beyond the reach of mortal eye." [6]

With the purchase of Louisiana and the news that "the British were threatening to set up shop in the Northwest"[7] Jefferson planned on sending a military exploratory expedition westward to secure the Oregon country for the United States. In 1802 Jefferson informed Captain Meriwether Lewis that he would command the group and that one of the purposes of the expedition would be that it would give "the American people a conviction that

---

[5] Edward Kowrach, *Mie. Charles Pandosy, O.M.I.:A Missionary of the Northwest*, 63
[6] The Avalon Project website, Thomas Jefferson First Inaugural Address
[7] Stephen Ambrose, *Undaunted Courage*, 75

Oregon was theirs and this conviction was more important than the claim."[8]

In 1818 the British and American governments agreed on the forty-ninth north parallel, from the Great Lakes to the Continental Divide, as the boundary between British and American territories. This agreement also stated that both sides would jointly occupy the lands of the Northwest; this area was as far north as fifty-four degrees and forty minutes, south to Spanish California and east to the Continental Divide.

When Andrew Jackson became President, a growing interest in the Northwest was occurring and he asked the British, in 1831, to reopen negotiations of the area. When the request was rejected, Jackson then, "based on the 1792 discovery of the 'Oregon' River by Captain Gray…laid claim to all lands drained by the great river system, changing the river's name to 'Columbia'…to further support the claim of sovereignty over the lands drained by the river system."[9]

US Navy Lieutenant William Slacum was sent to the Northwest with orders to secure firsthand information about the coastal areas of Oregon and California. Upon his return he recommended, in 1837, to both President Martin Van Buren and Congress that the forty-ninth north parallel should be the minimum

---

[8] Bernard DeVoto, *The Journals of Lewis and Clark*, lviii
[9] John Hemphill, *West Pointer and Early Washington: The Contributions of the U.S. Military Academy Graduates to the Development of the Washington Territory, from the Oregon Trail to the Civil War 1834-1864*, 18

northern border that the United States should demand because it would place the Puget Sound region in American territory.[10]

In 1842 President John Tyler sent a confidential communication to Congress recommending the US should claim the entire Columbia River drainage system and place the boundary at fifty-four degrees and forty minutes north parallel. Two years later his successor seemed to agree with him.

At the time James Polk was inaugurated as President he spoke "that our domain extends from ocean to ocean"[11] and that it was his duty "to assert and maintain by all Constitutional means the right of the United States to that portion of our territory which lies beyond the Rocky Mountains. Our title to the country of Oregon is 'clear and unquestionable,' and that our people are preparing to perfect that title by occupying it with their wives and children."[12]

The British reaction to such a strong statement was to send a warship to the Oregon country in order to safeguard their interests. Because of this movement, and discussions about the Texas problem, Polk now risked fighting two wars; one with Mexico and the other against the British in the Northwest. The President resolved to maintain a firm but prudent course of action due to the on-going negotiations over the boundary dispute issue.

In late August 1845, Polk ordered all US troops to leave the Northwest and to reinforce the command of Zachary Taylor around

---

[10] Ibid.
[11] The Avalon Project website, James Polk Inaugural Address
[12] Ibid

Corpus Christi. If war came to the Northwest then Polk would have no regular troops to defend that frontier.[13]

With no troops in the Northwest and negotiations at a standstill nearly eight months later Congress, on April 23, 1846, voted to end joint occupancy in one year regardless of what might happen with negotiations. Whatever the outcome might be Britain thought about war over the Oregon question.

War was declared against Mexico in May of that year and soon the British came back to the negotiations. By June 12 the two governments had agreed on the boundary between the U.S. and Canada. The boundary would run along "the 49th parallel to the Strait of San Juan de Fuca, ceding to Britain all of Vancouver Island and granting her unrestricted navigation of the Columbia River until 1859."[14] No one foresaw that the Treaty of Washington would lead, thirteen years later to, another test of strength in the Northwest.

After the return of the Lewis and Clark expedition the trickle of settlers did not cause the various Indian tribes of Oregon Territory much concern because they believed that the whites were few and did not have any designs on their land. But the trickle of whites became a steady flow and anger against them amounted to sporadic and unorganized fighting.

Missionaries were among the first group of people trying to establish control over the area. Doctor Marcus Whitman and Henry

---

[13] John Eisenhower, *So Far from God: The U.S. war with Mexico, 1846-1848*, 35
[14] Ibid., 68

Spalding, along with their wives were the first to settle in the area. They were followed by Elkanah Walker and Cushing Eells, and their wives, being positioned north of the first missions.

Soon Catholics came to establish missions around the Whitman mission. This started to cause problems, envy and disdain with Narcissa Whitman as she wrote, on August 23, 1842:

> *Romanism* [derogatory name for Catholicism] *stalks abroad on our right hand and on our left, and with daring effrontery, boasts that she is to prevail and possess the land. I ask, must it be so?... The zeal and energy of her priests are without parallel, and many, both white men and Indians, wander after the beasts. Two are in the country below us, and two far above in the mountains. One of the latter is to return this fall to Canada, the States and the eastern world for a large reinforcement. How true—"while men slept, the enemy came and sowed tares." Had a pious, devoted minister, a man of talent, come into the country and established himself at Vancouver, to human appearance the moral aspect of this country would not be the same as it is now; at least, we think Papacy would not have gained such a footing.*[15]

When emigration became intolerable to some tribes, the Cayuse War started in 1847 with the killings of Marcus Whitman and others because it was believed that Marcus Whitman had poisoned sick Indians and the belief that Indian medicine men who failed to cure their patients were themselves destined to die.

Father John Brouillet was the first outsider to arrive at the mission after the attack. He and Joseph Stanfield, who had been spared during the attack because he was French, buried the bodies.

Father Brouillet then went to search for Henry Spalding to tell him what had happened and that Spalding's life was

---

[15] Narcissa Whitman, *The letters of Narcissa Whitman 1836-1847*, 136

endangered. Brouillet found Spalding and urged him to get out of danger for which Spalding thanked him and made his escape toward The Dalles.

Once out of danger Spalding, and for the rest of his life, accused the Catholics as the main cause of the attack on the Whitmans and the start of the Cayuse War. Despite evidence to the contrary Spalding's accusations were accepted as truthful by many Protestant groups.

A group of Cayuse Indians agreed to go to Oregon City in order to convince the whites that the war leaders were dead. However, these men were arrested, tried and convicted on May 27, 1850. Upon being found guilty the group asked to see a priest for baptism and entry into the Catholic Church. On June 3 they were baptized and hanged. The war was considered finished.[16]

The war caused much change to the missionary movement. For the Protestants all missions were closed and the missionaries were recalled. This left the Catholic missions, as predicted by Narcissa Whitman, to 'prevail and posses the land.' It was also the only faith that the Indians generally trusted.

War upon the whites did nothing to stop the growing tide of immigrants and many tribes regretted not taking place in the Cayuse War in order to stop the Manifest Destiny of the United States. While many tribes did nothing to stop the stream of settlers, others took a more active role by attacking westward emigrants.

---

[16] Wilfred P. Schoenberg, S.J., *A History of the Catholic Church in the Pacific Northwest 1743-1983*, 128-129

1851-1854: Setting the stage

With the northern boundary issue concluded Americans began to settle in the newly obtained land. The Army was ordered back into the Northwest and this task was given to the Fourth U.S. Infantry Regiment. On September 22, 1852 the majority of the unit landed near the Army's Fort Vancouver. The rest arrived the following year.

To better deal with the administration of this new land a bill to create Washington Territory was introduced, in Congress, in 1853. President Millard Fillmore signed the act on March 2 passing responsibility for establishing the territory and its administration to the incoming President.

After Congress created the new territory it was up to the new President to decide who would be the first governor. Because of Isaac Stevens helpfulness in winning the presidency Franklin Pierce not only appointed him the governor of the new territory[17] but also Superintendent of Indian Affairs for the territory. Later, Stevens was appointed to lead the survey team for a northern railroad route across the Northwest.

Stevens gave first priority to the survey and started westward from Saint Paul, Minnesota. As they moved through Yakama[18] country they met Chief Kamiakin and offered him presents as a token of goodwill. Kamiakin refused the gifts

---

[17] Abraham Lincoln turned down the offer to be governor
[18] The spelling is correct for the tribe. The spelling of "Yakima" refers to the city

explaining that the British told him long ago of how the Americans would come into their land, offer them presents and say that they had just bought the land. Stevens stated that this was not the case.

From the start Kamiakin was opposed to the intrusion of the whites and had "kept [a] strict watch over his dominions and never permitted a white man, excepting Catholic Priests, to obtain a foothold within his realm."[19] He traveled from tribe to tribe warning them of the dangers of letting whites settle on their lands.

Units of the Fourth US Infantry were ordered to the strategic Fort Dalles, which was named in 1849 by Major Osborne Cross of the Regiment of Mounted Rifles as one of the two proper locations where a post might be built; the other being at the Hudson's Bay Company's Fort Vancouver. The location of the fort was chosen because it was near a trading and fishing hub for the local Indians.[20]

Prior to the Fourth occupying Fort Dalles a woman named Hamilton took up residence but had been warned by Kamiakin that if she stayed then her life would be endangered. With the arrival of the Army Kamiakin sent word to the fort that Hamilton had been

warned to get out of the country or else be killed. With this notice the post commander, Major Gabriel Rains, ordered Hamilton to leave her claim. This small action left Kamiakin with the integrity

---

[19] Granville Haller, *The Dismissal of Major Granville O. Haller of the Regular Army of the United States by order of the Secretary of War in Special Orders, No. 331, of July 25th, 1863*, 42

[20] Pricilla Knuth, *"Pictureque" Frontier: The Army's Fort Dalles*, 6-7

of his domain and a bolder determination to get rid of any whites who settled in his country.

It has been said that if Rains had ordered a guard to protect Hamilton and sent a message to Kamiakin saying that Hamilton was there to stay it would have brought the settlement issue between only the Yakama Indians and the Army. Instead it gave Kamiakin the time needed to gather other tribes in a joint war against the United States.[21]

In April, 1853 Father Charles Pandosy wrote a letter to Father Toussaint Mesplie of The Dalles warning of an Indian movement to drive out the whites. In part, the letter said:

> *A chief of the Upper Nez Perce has killed 30 head of cattle at a feast given to the nation...This feast was given in order to unite the hearts of all the Indians together, to make declarations of war against the Americans. Through the whole course of the Winter I have heard the same thing—that the Cayuse and the Nez Perces have united themselves for war...All the Indians on the left bank of the Columbia, from the Blackfeet to the Chinook, inclusive, are to assemble at the Cayuse country. All on the right bank, through the same extent of country, are to assemble on the Simcoe including those from Nesqually and its vicinity. The cause of the war is, that the American are going to seize their lands.*[22]

The letter was passed to the regional military command and caused much anxiety in the area. However, military authorities outside the region decided to do nothing with the report and maintained normal operations.

Father Pandosy's letter was later included in a report to the 35th Congress with the following words added:

---

[21] Kowrach, *Charles Pandosy*, 219
[22] Ibid., 75

This grave and startling information so fearfully verified since, was promptly communicated to Major Alvord, who reported it to General Hitchcock, the then commanding officer of the military department of this coast. Major[Benjamin] *Alvord was censured as an alarmist, and Father Pandosy was treated in the same manner by his superior.*[23]

On January 29, 1854 Rains wrote to his superiors that:

The time has arrived when it becomes necessary to determine the question of peace or war between the citizens of the United States and Indian tribes on this frontier, east of the "Cascades" and west of the Rocky Mountains.
Indian complaints have been brought from time to time that the white men are locating on their land, against their will, and that without respect to their individual possessions, or property, or priority of title of Indian claimants.[24]

The Army passed through the year with routines of drills, inspections and patrolling the region and it also began to build roads. Lacking soldiers the Army did not operate in the interior of the Columbia Plateau. There was very little reason to do so because most of the emigrants along the Oregon Trail settled along the costal region and the entire white population of the territory, at the end of 1854, was less than 5,500.[25]

With the surveying work over Governor Stevens told the territorial legislature, in December 1854, that making treaties with the Indians would be his next primary activity. The main purpose of these treaties was to get the Indians to give up any claims to

---

[23] Ibid., 75-76
[24] Donald Shannon, *The Boise Massacre on the Oregon Trail,* 44
[25] Hemphill, *West Pointers,* 29

their lands so that white settlers could move in under the Donation Land Claim Act of 1850.[26]

Realizing that the Indians would resist being moved from their traditional lands the Indian Bureau gave instructions for the number of treaties and reservations to be kept at a minimum. The Bureau also realized that enmity between tribes would further create problems of co-locating tribes on the same reservation. It further gave instructions that the reservations were to be in remote locations as to separate the Indians from the areas that whites would settle.

This would not be the first attempt at getting the various Indian tribes to move to reservations. In 1851 attempts were made with various tribes along the lower Columbia River, Willapa Bay and Cowlitz River region. Treaties were signed but they were never ratified by the US Senate because they failed to provide the agreement that the tribes could be removed from the area whites wanted to settle. Stevens was determined that his treaties would be ratified.[27]

1855: Treaties and War

In late August 1854 word reached Fort Dalles that the twenty-member emigrant party of Alexander Ward were killed by Snake Indians of the Northern Shoshoni, along the part of the

---

[26] Donation Land Claim Act of 1850- Gave 320 acres for every unmarried white male, over the ager of 18 and 640 acres for every couple who arrived in Oregon Territory before December 1, 1850. Anyone who arrived after the cutoff date and before 1854 were allowed half the amount stated. Claimants must live on the land for 4 years to own the land outright.

[27] Hemphill, *West Pointers*, 29-30

Oregon Trail that was close to the Hudson's Bay Company's Fort Boise. Major Rains ordered Major Granville Haller to take his command and aid any survivors and to punish the Indians responsible for this.

Because of discharges and desertions the two companies assigned to Fort Dalles had a total of fifty-six soldiers. Haller took twenty-six of them with him to carry out his assignment. However, the citizens of The Dalles thought his command was too small and formed a company of thirty-nine volunteers, under the command of Nathan Olney, who followed him and reported for duty. This mixed unit was also joined by a few warriors of the Nez Percés and Umatilla Indians that offered their services.

Upon arriving at the massacre site the command discovered a grisly scene. Bodies were found to be beaten badly and stripped of clothing. Mrs. Ward, for example, was found in center of the camp and in front of her *lay the crisped bodies of her children, who had doubtless, been burnt alive, and the mother forced to witness it.*[28]

Haller ordered the bodies buried. The command then returned to Fort Dalles because the Indians had long since fled into the mountains and it was too late in the season to go find them.

The following spring General John Wool, commanding the Department of the Pacific, ordered Haller to mount another expedition and return to the Ward massacre site. Haller's orders

---

[28] Anne Bird, *Boise, the peaceful valley*, 82

were to find and punish the Indians responsible and this time he commanded 150 men.

He reached the Fort Boise area on July 15 and the next day talks were held with around 200 hundred Indians that were gathered. During the talks it was determined that four of the participants of the Ward killing were among those present. Haller ordered their arrest and brought before a military commission in which he reminded the commission that "the poor Indians cannot and should not be judged by the standard of the civilized and Christianized nations of the world."[29] However, they were tried and found guilty of the killings.

One of the Indians was shot while trying to escape but the other three were marched, on July 18, to the Ward site and the troops started to build gallows to carry out the sentence of the commission. The sentence was "read and interpreted to the Indians, who were placed in a wagon with ropes around their necks. The soldiers paraded at sundown, then the signal was given, the wagon drove from under the Indians, and they swung into eternity. The bodies were left handing until sunrise the next morning, and which time they were taken down and buried at the foot of the gallows."[30]

The bodies of the Ward party were also reburied because the wolves had dug them up during the winter. Once the burials were finished Haller, leaving the gallows standing, ordered a march and later established a supply depot on the Big Camash

---

[29] H. Dean Guie, *Bugles in the Valley: Garnett's Fort Simcoe,* 7
[30] Bird, *Boise,* 89

Prairie. From there the command travelled as far north as the headwaters of the Boise, Payette and Snake Rivers; to the east the Rocky Mountains and headwaters of the Missouri; to the south the Salmon Falls along the Snake River.

During this expedition, besides the killing of the four Indians, the command killed and hanged several more until the number of dead Indians equaled the number of dead whites. He caused the Snake Indians to flee from the area and many of them fled towards the Humboldt River in California and out of jurisdiction of Fort Dalles. The command returned home after covering a distance of around 1700 miles.

The treaty year of 1855 actually began in late December 1854 near Medicine Creek at the southern end of Puget Sound. Long before Governor Stevens arrived the locals assured the various tribes that the government would pay them well for their land. When the governor finally arrived he came with a draft treaty and maps ready for the Indians signatures and finalization.

Once this treaty was signed it was sent immediately to Washington, DC for ratification. It was approved in March 1855 and gave the governor the model to follow and the confidence to make further treaties.

Other councils were convened and it was in May 1855 that the first Walla Walla council started. By the time the council started the invited tribes had heard about the removals of tribes to reservations and Major Granville Haller's expedition into the Boise River area and his hangings of the Indians. The mood of the tribes had changed from friendliness, when Stevens first came with the railroad survey, to one of caution and even resentment towards the whites.

The council formally opened on May 29 and again Stevens was armed with maps and treaties waiting to be signed so he could send them to be ratified. A few days after the start Nez Perce Chief Lawyer was informed of a Cayuse "plot to massacre the Army escort and the Governor's party, followed by a surprise attack on Fort Dalles."[31] Lawyer quickly moved his lodge into the governor's camp thereby signaling other tribes that the Nez Perce firmly sided with the Americans.

After weeks of talk Stevens realized that there was a mounting opposition to the treaties because failure of the reservation plan would undo all the reservations that had already been created. Kamiakin, when asked to speak, replied "I have nothing to talk long about. I am tired. I am anxious to get back to my garden. That is all I have to say."[32] Nez Perce Chief Looking Glass questioned his tribe on why they were giving away their lands. Together these two men provided a rallying point for holdouts of other tribes.

In the end the tribes signed the treaty with the last being on June 11. When Kamiakin signed the treaty Stevens said to him, "Tell the chiefs if they don't sign this treaty they will walk in blood knee deep."[33] Kamiakin said nothing when he signed but

---

[31] Robert Burns, SJ, *The Jesuits and the Indian Wars of the Northwest*, 37
[32] Kowrach, *Charles Pandosy*, 85
[33] Ibid., 87

when he turned from the table his lips were covered in blood from biting them.

From the Americans point of view the treaty was a success because the various tribes gave up large tracts of land. While the treaty stated that it would only become valid once ratified Stevens immediately announced that the area east of the Cascades was opened for settlement. This event greatly disturbed the Indians and they now saw the wisdom of Kamiakin and turned to him for advice.

Kamiakin told them during the winter time that the Cascades would be closed and that the whites, on the west side of the mountains, could not come to the aid of the whites on the east side. He urged them to start to gather ammunition and when winter came to kill all whites who were on their territory. Finally, he reminded them of the Indians of the Willamette Valley and how they had been put on reservations and not been paid because the treaties with the whites were hollow.[34] With this advice runners were sent out to all tribes and plans were made for war upon the whites during the winter.

The treaty caused problems for the Army. Many officers were sympathetic toward the Indians. Men like "Major Rains discouraged squatting until the Indian title to the soil could be extinguished."[35] This often angered the settlers who "insisted that

---

[34] Haller, *Dismissal*, 43
[35] Kowrach, *Charles Pandosy*, 218

the treaties ought to be regarded as actually in force so that whites could enter Indian country."[36]

In September 1855 gold was discovered in the Colville region causing a rush of miners to the area through increasingly hostile Indian territory. Because of the rumors that miners had assaulted Yakama Chief Teias' daughter some miners were hunted and killed in retaliation; soon the Yakamas killed several more miners and the body count ran up to twenty.[37]

Indian Sub-Agent Andrew Bolon was on his way to join Stevens when he heard about the killings. Since the Yakamas were his charge he traveled into Yakama country to find out the cause of the killings and, if possible, arrest the murderers in hopes of bringing them to trial in The Dalles.

On the fateful morning of September 23 the Yakama Indian Wah-tan-kon warned those who were with him:

Last night in my waking-sleep I saw a White man. I know not how I saw him, but he was there before my eyes as I now see you. Blood was upon him! He was all stained with blood! Blood on his face; blood on his clothes. He was not good to see. Listen well to my words; what I am telling you! If you do not, you will know sorrow. Trouble will follow and overtake you on the trail.

Should you see a White man today, if you meet one, do not bother him. Let him alone to go his way, to live his own life. Put no blood upon him. You will bring evil to our lives if you do. Remember what I am telling you.[38]

The warning fell upon deaf ears and war would soon fall upon the Yakama tribe.

---

[36] Edmund Becher, *History, Government and Resources of the Spokane area*, 37
[37] Burns, *The Jesuits*, 126
[38] Lucullus McWhorter, *Tragedy of the Wahk-Shum*, 32

In order to find out why Agent Bolon was delayed in his return, Major Haller sent an Indian spy into Yakama country who later returned with great difficulty. While waiting for his spy to return Haller learned of an old Indian woman who had slipped away from her tribe and informed the military not only of Bolon's death but that the Yakamas had sent "runners to inform their allies of their danger, and threw out scouts to observe the movements of the soldiers at Fort Dalles, and took every precaution to keep those Indians not disposed for war, from communicating with the white people."[39] Haller's spy, upon his return, confirmed Bolon's death.

Bolon was travelling south towards Fort Dalles in company with several Yakama members. Upon stopping for the night Bolon was attacked and killed. Both he and his horse were burned.

Upon learning the details of Bolon's demise Haller forwarded the details to Major Rains. He then prepared Fort Dalles' two companies of about 100 soldiers, comprised mostly of new recruits, and a howitzer for an immediate march northwards. Orders from Fort Vancouver never came.

With the Army officially doing little to investigate the death of Agent Bolon and to bring back the murderers for justice, Acting Governor of Washington Territory Charles Mason demanded that the Army send troops, from Fort Dalles, into Yakama territory and take into custody the murderers.

Rains then ordered Haller to take only one company with him and then wrote a letter back to the governor stating the he had

---

[39] Ibid., 37

ordered into the filed, a company of eighty-four men from Fort Dalles, O.T., all mounted, and with provisions on pack mules for one month, to proceed without delay and sweep through the Yakima country [and to] *inquire into the safety of Agent Bolon, who has been absent an unusual length of time...*[40]

Haller, realizing the danger and despite a chance at a court martial, ignored the order for only one company and collected his entire force of 102 men, a howitzer and supplies. On October 2 the command crossed the Columbia River and headed northwards.

On the first night one of Haller's spies returned and told him that Chief Kamiakin had "collected more warriors than he was able to designate by numbers, and that a force double [Haller's] size would never be able to get back."[41] Acting under Rains' orders Haller decided to press on because he "and even some Yakama leaders expected a parley rather than a fight."[42]

Around 3 PM on October 6 as the expedition came down from the Simcoe Mountains, into the Yakama Valley and approached the bottom of the Toppenish Creek they saw some Indians concealing themselves behind oak and cottonwood trees as a chief was giving signals to them. The warriors responded with yells and thus gave away their exact position and their approximate numbers.

---

[40] Frant Gilbert, *Historic Sketches of Walla Walla, Whitman, Columbia and Garfield Counties, Washington Territory*, 162
[41] Haller, *Dismissal*, 38
[42] Carl Schlicke, "Long Road to Vindication for Accused Northwest Soldier", 25

Troops were deployed for battle as the howitzer was set up and commenced firing while the supply train was hurried up and guarded as soldiers reached the ford only to find themselves unsupported by other troops. They managed to return to the line with only some minor wounds.

Once everything was ready Haller ordered Captain David Russell's company to advance down a foliaged steep bank near the front line. They moved undetected and flanked the Indian line which drove over 200 warriors from the surrounding area giving the command time to collect its casualties and move, in the dark, north about a mile to a better position.

During the night the howitzer fired several shots but stopped when Haller called out to them loudly to cease firing. When he went to investigate the reason for their action the howitzer crew stated that two mounted Indians rode up to them and seeing their mistake turned their horses around and fled.

One of the fortunate outcomes of this unauthorized firing was that the medical staff, who were out in the field bringing back the wounded, recognized Haller's voice. Having called back to Haller for a guide they were successfully escorted back to camp. Without the firing of the howitzer the medical team would have continued to walk into the Indian line.

The next morning found the expedition occupying an ancient burial ground that was on a sloping terrain scattered with sandy spots and stony outcroppings and surrounded by over 600 warriors and also a dead Indian and his horse in front of the howitzer position. Several attempts by Indians were made to break the defense perimeter by having war parties crawl up close, construct barricades to protect themselves from musket fire and then attacking the soldiers with whatever weapon they carried. It was often by bayonet charges that these attacks were driven off.

Overnight the recruits had become veterans and were learning how to use their bayonets effectively but were still wasting ammunition on foes both real and imagined. To the officers and men who looked over the field of battle it was clear that reinforcements were coming to help the Indians and many troopers wondered if they would survive another day.

Haller realized that they had not enough food and ammunition to last until reinforcements arrived and that it would be foolish to think that his command could defeat the enemy. He wrote a letter to be carried by a runner to Fort Dalles at the first chance which, among other things, said "I am thinking of retreat, before a retreat becomes impracticable."[43]

That night the Indians abandoned the fight in order to return refreshed and to finish off Haller's command the next morning. Haller ordered his command to pack up fast "and supplies were burned or abandoned and cattle and unneeded horses turned loose before the command moved out."[44] They moved to Toppenish Creek where they watered for the first time since the fighting began. Once refreshed with water they climbed Toppenish Ridge that zig-zagged so much that the forty-man rear guard got lost in the dark.

---

[43] Guie, *Bugle*, 10
[44] Schlicke, Long Road, 25

In the morning a running fight began for several miles but the soldiers were able to keep the enemy at a distance. During the day the mules carrying the howitzer could no longer keep up so the howitzer was covered with leaves and abandoned. In addition, any other unneeded packs and supplies were jettisoned and the march continued when it was dark.

That night they found the missing rear guard, met with a company of reinforcements and arrived back at Fort Dalles on the tenth. The command counted five dead and seventeen wounded.

This Indian victory moved tribes that were wavering into war against the whites and Kamiakin became the leader of this effort. In a last ditch effort to avoid war Father Pandosy, whom Kamiakin trusted, gave a speech to the Indians warning them of the evils of war. The Indians, heeding the speech, asked Father Pandosy to write a letter to Haller describing their grievances against the Americans for taking their land. The letter dated October 7, 1855 ended with:

Write this, Father Pandosy, to the soldiers and the Americans so that they can give you an answer, and let us know what they think. If they do not answer, it is because they want war; we are at this moment 1,050 men assembled. Some only will go to battle, but as soon as the war is begun the news will spread among all our nations and in a few days we will be more than 10,000. If peace is wanted, we will consent to it, but it must be written to us so we may know about it.[45]

The letter was sent by an Indian messenger who could not find Haller. Upon the messengers return Father Pandosy sent a

---

[45] Kowrach, *Charles Pandosy*, 96-97

copy of it to another priest and left the original at Ahtanum Mission in hopes that the soldiers would find it.

The repulse of Haller's command brought reaction from both the military and political leaders. Various settlements recruited militia ordering one company to rescue Governor Stevens' party and also demanding 4,000 regular soldiers be sent into Yakama country and punish the Indians. [46]Major Rains stripped the forts at Vancouver and Steilacoom of most of its troops and marched them to Fort Dalles in order to mount an offensive against the Indians and to punish them for their actions.

The governor of Oregon, believing that a large force was necessary to protect settlers from the disputed territory, called out a large force of volunteers and commissioned its leader with the rank of general. Some of the volunteers moved northwards into Cayuse country and erected a fort on the Umatilla River and called it Fort Henrietta after Haller's wife for the kindness that she showed in helping to raise the unit.

The rest of the volunteers were sent to Fort Dalles where Rains threw up many obstacles because the commanding officer of the volunteers had a superior rank. The delay was enough to see the first snowfall in the region causing the unit at Fort Henrietta to realize they would not be getting any support soon and thus necessitating their movement back to Fort Dalles before they would be surrounded by hostiles.

---

[46] Burns, *The Jesuits*, 128

The command was finally ready to move in late October because the Acting Governor of Washington Territory gave Rains the rank of general of the volunteers. While the dispute over the volunteers continued Chief Kaskala, of the Qascopams, came to visit Haller and reported that Kamiakin had advised all the tribes to bring their people and join the war against the whites. If not, Kamiakin warned, them that they will become slaves of the whites and their property taken. Kaskala, being afraid that Chief Kamiakin would kill all the whites, asked Haller what he should do.

Haller asked Kaskala if he noticed that after fishing for salmon one year the next year's run was less to which Kaskala responded negatively. Haller then explained that even if all the whites were killed this year that "the White man will wipe out the last Indian, for making war [and] just like the salmon run each season, you will find as many more Whites, the next season coming into your country."[47]

Upon hearing this Kaskala told Haller he and his people would not join Kamiakin. Haller then told him that in case war did come south of the Columbia River that he should bring all his people to the Fort. Haller also asked, in order to show good faith, that a number of warriors, familiar with Yakama culture join the expedition; this was agreed to.

The command left Fort Dalles on October 30 with about 700 regular and Washington and Oregon volunteer troops mustered

---

[47] Ibid., 233

into federal service. The expedition marched only eight miles in the first three days. By November 9 they had reached the area known as the Two Buttes located near Union Gap. Here Indians occupied one of the Buttes and Rains halted his force in order to allow the volunteers to start the fighting. The volunteers took a dim view of this and thought that the regulars should do most of the fighting.

Very little action occurred and the commander of the Oregon troops sent word to Rains that he was going to camp along the banks of the Yakama River. Haller, seeing little going on volunteered to send his company in order to drive off the Indians from the Butte; the offer was declined.

That evening the command marched to the Yakama River and made camp. Haller, among other officers, took their companies and rushed the Butte because they saw that those soldiers who had engaged the Indians during the day were driven back into camp in confusion. They drove off the Indians and secured that position for the night.

On November 13 the troops reached and examined the now abandoned Catholic mission at Ahtanum Creek. Upon seeing the letter that Father Pandosy had left for Haller, Major Rains ordered the mission destroyed after gunpowder was found buried in the garden.[48] It was falsely assumed that the priests were supplying ammunition to the Indians.

---

[48] The mission was looted by soldiers before it was burned. Many of these ill gotten items have become heirlooms. Other items were rescued and sent to St. Peter's Church in The Dalles. These items have been misplaced and lost.

Major Rains left his own letter which stated: *We will…war forever, until not a Yakima breathes in the land he calls his own…Our warriors in the field are many-as you must see- but if not enough, a thousand for every one…will be sent to hunt you and kill you; and my kind advice to you…is to scatter yourselves among the Indian tribes more peaceful and there forget you were ever Yakimas.*[49]

With the snow starting and little to show except for the destruction of St. Joseph's Mission and a few supplies for the Indians the command headed back to Fort Dalles to settle in for winter quarters. They stopped at Haller's battlefield, near Toppenish Creek on November 15 to rebury the bones, that were uncovered by wolves, of the soldiers who had died there and rendered them full military honors.

The whole command marched into Fort Dalles a few days later. It was then that charges and counter-charges were made against many of the officers in trying to lay blame for the failure of the expedition. However, no trials were convened against any officer because General James Wool, commanding the Department of the Pacific, said he didn't have enough officers to seat a court.

War came to the Puget Sound region on October 27 when militia forces were attacked and Chief Leschi was blamed for this incident. The next day members of the Muckleshoots attacked and killed three families along the White River.[50]

Blockhouses were built and volunteers joined the war. Between November 4-7 volunteers under the command of Captain

---

[49] Kowrach, *Charles Pandosy*, 104
[50] Murray Morgan, *Puget's Sound: A narrative of early Tacoma and the southern sound*, 100-101

Maurice Maloney battled bands of Puyallup, Nisqually and Squaxon warriors around the Puyallup River before the Indians finally broke off the engagements and scattered.

Following the fight around the Puyallup River troops under the command of Lieutenant William Slaughter were stationed at Brannon's Prairie. During the night of December 4, under the cover of a heavy fog, Klickitat warriors, under the command of Chief Kanaskat, surrounded the camp. They then fired a volley before retreating into the darkness.

The Army's casualties were 3 enlisted men wounded but Lieutenant Slaughter had been killed.

The rest of the year brought attacks and counter-attacks from both the Indians and whites. Causalities were often low for both sides as they waited out the year and waiting to see what the new year would bring.

1856-1857: A troubled peace

On January 21, 1856 the Ninth Infantry Regiment, under the command of Colonel George Wright arrived at Fort Vancouver. Wright, being the senior officer in the district, assumed command. The governor of Oregon withdrew his volunteer forces deeming that an adequate force was available to conduct war against the Indians.

Rumors abounded that Indians were going to attack the town of Seattle. The town prepared themselves and the naval ship *USS Decatur* detached some sailors and marines to man a howitzer for the attack. The attack came on January 26 and was beaten back. The attacking warriors retreated that evening in defeat.

The next day Lieutenant Colonel Silas Casey took command of the Puget Sound district and began planning operations against the Indians.

That spring saw US forces searching for the Indians and engaging them where ever they were found. The US also disrupted the Indian way of life, by setting up more blockhouses at key rivers and prairies, and many warriors soon grew tired of the war and took their families away from the conflict.

The last large scale battle west of the Cascades took place at Connell's Prairie on March 4. Two companies of volunteers were sent to Connell's Prairie to establish a ferry and a blockhouse. Before they could start their assigned tasks they were attacked by about 150 Klickitats. The volunteers countercharged and the Indians were driven off.

Without a peace conference or treaty the war in the Puget Sound region was declared over on May 11, 1856. [51]

During the early part of March Wright started to move his command downriver from Fort Vancouver to Fort Dalles. On March 27, hearing of Indians attacking Fort Cascasdes, Wright commanded a two pronged relief effort which resulted in the attackers being defeated and many of the Indians escaping.

With this attack in mind General Wool ordered Wright to prosecute the war against the Yakamas and to force them to sue for

---

[51] Hemphill, *West Pointers*, 52

peace. Wright moved his forces forward at the end of April. At the Nechess River Wright established Camp Nechess River and waited for the river to subside so that they could cross it.

While waiting for the river to lower Chiefs Owhi and Teias came across the river to talk to Wright. The Chiefs professed they were tired of war and wanted peace. They also told Wright that the treaties that Governor Stevens forced upon them were the main cause of the conflict. Colonel Wright listened to them but made it clear that they must lay down their arms and become peaceful.

The Chiefs agreed to return in five days with all the stolen goods and comply with all the demands. They never returned and it was reported that Kamiakin, and his followers, had gone east to the area of the Spokane tribe.

Leaving a small force to garrison Camp Nachess, Wright set out on June 17 with a force of about 450 men to penetrate the Yakama heartland and to show that previously thought of safe areas were no place to hide from US forces.

The command returned to Camp Nachess on July 21 and it was soon abandoned after Wright ordered Major Robert Garrett to maintain operations in the area and build Fort Simcoe. With Kamiakin, and his followers, out of the region the conflict had come to an uneasy truce.

With the hostilities in the Yakama region coming to a close the Army looked at establishing more posts to keep the various tribes under a vigilant eye. These included the building of Fort Simcoe (commanded by Major Robert Garnett), in the Yakama Valley, Fort Walla Walla (commanded by Lieutenant Colonel

Edward Steptoe), near the Whitman mission site, and Fort Bellingham (commanded by Captain George Pickett), close to Canada.

On September 11 the Second Walla Walla Council was convened with some of the important Indian chiefs not attending and the mood was that the treaties should be cancelled and settlers kept off their lands. Governor Stevens went on the defensive and countered that the treaties must be kept and that Indians who committed hostile acts against settlers must be turned over to the whites; he did not answer questions about what should happen to settlers who committed hostile acts against Indians.[52]

The Council ended on September 17 with nothing accomplished and the Governor's party left the next day for The Dalles. They were attacked and the volunteers who guarded the Governor were able to keep the attackers at a distance. The next day forces sent by Steptoe drove back the attackers and escorted the party to The Dalles.

Governor Stevens criticized the end of the war and Colonel Wright on November 21, 1856 by saying: *I now make the direct issue with Colonel Wright; that he has made concession to the Indians which he had no authority to make; that, by so doing, he has done nothing but to get the semblance of a peace, and that by his acts he has, in measure, weakened the influence of the service having the authority to make treaties and having charge of friendly Indians. He has, in my judgment, abandoned his own duty, which*

---

[52] Hemphill, *West Pointers*, 57

was to reduce the Indians to submission, and has trenched upon and usurped a portion of mine.[53]

In 1857 the Army's major activity was building of new forts to protect the settlers in the Territory. Also, General Wool, commanding the Department of the Pacific, requested reassignment and was replaced by General Newman Clarke in June.

The buildings of forts were generally inadequate for the protection and defense of settlers in the region. In fact beyond the building of Forts Simcoe and Walla Walla there were no further plans in keeping a watchful eye on the interior regions. The Territory was "in an almost wholly defenseless condition, at the very time when a general Indian rising was most feared."[54]

Clarke visited the region and conferred with his officers and other government officials. Upon his return to San Francisco he wrote Army Headquarters, on November 4, 1857, stating

The superintendent [of Indian affairs] *informed me that the treaties had never been confirmed and it would be impolite to confirm them, and his influence would be used to prevent it.*

Agreeing with him as to the impolicy of enforcing them, at a hazard of a serious war, I determined with his approval to remove distrust, by letting them [the Indians] know that the treaties were non-effective, [and] *issued instructions to commanding officers to that end.*[55]

---

[53] Grant, *Historical Sketches*, 211 [54] Burns, *The Jesuits*, 60
[55] US Congress, *Annual message from the President to the two Houses of Congress, 1858*, 331-332

As early as 1856 the Army's policy was that *no emigrant or other white person, except for the Hudson's Bay Company, or persons having ceded rights from the Indians, will be permitted to settle or to remain in Indian country, or on land not settled or not confirmed by the Senate and approved by the President of the United States.*

These orders are not, however, to apply to miners engaged in collecting gold at Colville mines. [56]

However, the settlers didn't like this continuing policy and complained to Washington Territory Legislature which issued a resolution, on January 15, 1858, saying

Whereas certain officers of the United States Army, commanding in the country of Walla Walla, have unlawfully assumed to issue orders prohibiting citizens of this Territory from settling in certain portions thereof, and in accordance with said orders have driven citizens and settlers from their claims and homes acquired under the laws of the United States, to their great injury.

Therefore be it resolved by the legislative assembly of the Territory of Washington that, in our opinion the said orders are without the authority of law, and that the acts done under said orders are a high handed outrage upon the rights and liberties of the American people.

Resolved, That the Governor be requested to give the proper authorities at Washington all necessary information on the subject of the outrageous usurpation of the military over the civil authority

Resolved, That we believe the above usurpation to be the very worst form of martial law, proclaimed by tyrants not having feeling the common with us, nor interests identified with ours...[57]

---

[56] Grant, *Historical Sketches*, 211
[57] Benjamin Manring, *Conquest of the Coeur D' Alenes, Spokanes and Palouses*, 50-51

This resolution was sent to the War Department but did not result in any change of policies.

1858: Disaster for the tribes

In early 1858 General Clarke received word that the Mormons were arming the Indians around the Snake River and the Mormons could supply the tribes of the Northwest with everything they wished for. Clarke also received a letter, from a George Gibbs, who reported

A very curious statement was recently made me by some of the Indians near Steilacoom. They said that the Klikatats had told them that Choosuklee, (Jesus Christ,) had recently appeared on the other side of the mountains; that he was after awhile coming here, when the whites would be sent out of the country, and all would be well for themselves. It needed only a little reflection to connect this second advent with the visit of Brigham Young to the Flathead and Nez Percés country.[58]

On January 12, 1858 orders, from the Department of the Pacific, were written to Lieutenant Colonel Steptoe stating:

The general [General Clarke, commanding the Department] wishes you to be deeply impressed with the importance of obtaining early and full information in relation to the Indian tribes in your vicinity, and south and east towards Fort Hall and the Salmon river.

Information from various sources and points on the frontier leads him to the conclusion that through the Mormons the Indians are being inclined to hostility, and that a conflict in Utah may be the signal for trouble on the frontier, and it is not improbable that the Mormons may move north.

---

[58] US Congress, *Annual Message, 1858*, 335

He wishes you to be prepared in advance for either contingency. Full and prompt report of all information, and your opinion founded thereon, is desired.[59]

Steptoe kept watch on the frontier and reported to Headquarters, on April 17, that settlers of the Colville area had petitioned for troops because they believed that their lives and property were threatened. He also reported that Indians had raided the area around Fort Walla Walla, managed capture livestock that belonged to the Army and that the Oregon Trail immigrants did not reach the Snake River Plains until August so that the Army could protect them when the command returned from the Colville region.

On May 6 over 150 men and officers left the fort and instead of proceeding in a most direct route they made a wide detour towards the northeast. They went this way because the Snake River was high and where they wanted to cross was thought to be the easiest to traverse. Also, Chief Timothy, of the Nez Percé, was encamped at the place they wanted to cross and it was thought that he would provide help in moving the command across the creek. When they did cross one of Steptoe's Nez Percé scouts refused to cross the Snake because he learned that the Palouse Indians were waiting to attack and tried to warn Steptoe of this fact. Steptoe didn't give much thought to the warning and moved his troops across.

After the crossing Timothy sent his emissaries to Chief Tilcoax, of the Palouse, saying they soon would lose their territory,

---

[59] Ibid., 337

women and horses. Tilcoax hated the whites since the days of the Cayuse War and worked, like Kamiakin, to unify the tribes against the whites. Timothy also sent envoys to other tribes further north with the same message while telling the Nez Percé scouts to keep silent that Timothy wanted a fight with Tilcoax.[60]

On the night of the fifteenth Steptoe had heard that a large Indian force was gathering along his intended route and he ordered a doubling up of guards for the night. On Sunday, May 16, around 11AM a large force (numbers are estimated to be between 600-1200) of painted Indians blocked his path. Thinking that it was their intention to attack Steptoe quickly backtracked to a small lake.

The Indians followed Steptoe and taunted the soldiers "yelling, whooping, shaking scalps, and other such things over their heads, looking like so many fiends."[61] For the next three hours the Indians kept up the verbal assaults and then pulled back without a shot being fired from either side.

That night several chiefs, including Chief Garry of the Spokanes, met with Steptoe and wanted to know what he was doing there and if rumors were true that he was there to make war upon them. Steptoe answered that:

we were passing on to Colville, and had no hostile intentions towards the Spokanes, who had always been our friends, nor towards any other tribes who were friendly; that my chief aim in coming so far was to see the Indians and the white people at

---

[60] Clifford E. Trafzer and Richard D. Scheuerman, *Renegade Tribe: The Palouse Indians and the Invasion of the Inland Pacific Northwest*, 78
[61] Ibid., 79

Colville, and by friendly discussion with both, endeavor to strengthen their good feelings towards each other.[62]

The chiefs were satisfied with the answers but refused to offer aid or assistance in crossing the Spokane River. They also warned that the tribes were greatly excited by the presence of troops and that they "might not be able to restrain the warriors from making an attack."[63]

Seeing that nothing further would be accomplished by talking Steptoe moved his men to a more favorable position. Another conference with the chiefs was arranged and they asked him why he had brought the howitzers and brushed off his remarks about going to Colville by saying that he must have gotten lost on the route.

At sunset the Indians stopped their taunting and withdrew a distance from the Army camp. However, they did let it be known that they would have attacked that day if it wasn't a Sunday. Steptoe told his men to be ready for action and then called a council of war with his officers. No one slept that night as everyone knew that the situation was growing worse by the hour.

Before sunrise the command began its retreat southwards. The unit was strung out in a long column of five companies with 1,000 yards between each element. By the time they had barely moved three miles Indians appeared following them on their flanks and rear and painted for war.

---

[62] US Congress, *Annual Message, 1858*, 346
[63] Edmund Becher, *History, Government and Resources of the Spokane area*, 39

About this time Father Joseph Joset appeared from the Coeur d'Alene mission with the intent of trying to stop the battle. He found Steptoe on the move. Steptoe said that the conversation had to be made while the train was moving because the pack animals were too frightened for a long stop. During the conversation Steptoe lied to the priest and asserted that he was only going to Colville, that they were not looking for a fight and that they had not been given warning that they would not be allowed to cross the Spokane River.

Joset urged another meeting with the chiefs and Steptoe agreed. However, Joset could only find one chief that was willing to talk and that accomplished nothing. Before leaving the area Joset relayed a warning to Steptoe that the Palouses were about ready to attack.

The Palouse did not attack and Steptoe, determined to avoid fighting, ordered that fire should be returned only if a position was in danger of being overrun. This order hindered the men of the rear column when the Indians did finally make their attack. Finally, after being shot at and their position threatened, the rear guard returned fire having been made fully aware of the ammunition supply (each soldier carried only 40 rounds of ammunition).

Thus started ten hours of a running battle, which was marked by charges and counter-charges on each side, and each side had different objectives. To Steptoe his first and primary objective was to make sure his men were safe and that they made it back to Fort Walla Walla. His other goal was to hope that the scout he sent out the previous night had made it to the fort so that reinforcements could be brought up.

During the running fight Steptoe realized he had to stop, regroup and prepare for whatever might happen the following day. Looking around, at the present day battlefield near Rosalia, Washington, he saw what was the high ground of the area and successfully forced his command to the top of the hill and placed the baggage and wounded in the center. Tall grass added some concealment because soldiers could dismount, lie flat and present less of a target than they would on horseback. But the attacks kept coming and the position was threatened to be overran at least twice. Fortunately, for the soldiers by 8 PM the Indian attacks had ended giving the command time to regroup and plan for the next day.

The command was in serious trouble and everyone knew it. Troops had not eaten or drunk all day and they were tired, not having slept the previous night. The wounded cried for water which further unnerved the soldiers. Finally, "it was manifest that the loss of their officers and comrades began to tell upon the spirit of the soldiers; they were becoming discouraged, and not to be relied upon."[64]

Steptoe held another council of war with his officers and none of them doubted that their position would be lost the next day. Another thing that must have crossed Steptoe's mind was the fact that if they were defeated Fort Walla Walla would also go

---

[64] US Congress, *Annual Message, 1855*, 347

down in defeat because a lack of forces and supplies there. Finally, the entire interior of the Territory would be engulfed in war and no white settlement would be safe. Steptoe later reported that:

It was plain that the enemy would give the troops no rest during the night, and they would be still be further disqualified for stout resistance on the morrow, while the number of enemies would certainly be increased. I determined, for these reasons, to make a forced march to Snake river, about eighty-five miles distant, and secure the canoes in advance of the Indians who had already threatened to do the same in regard to us. After consulting with the officers, all of whom urged me to the step as the only means in their opinion of securing the safety of the command, I concluded to abandon every thing that might impede our march.[65]

The orders were given and everything that was not needed was to be abandoned to the Indians. Baggage and the dead were left on the hill and the howitzers buried; by 10 PM the troops quietly started to move off the hill, passed the Indian encampments and successfully made back to the fort without any further engagements around May 20.

General Clarke came to Fort Vancouver in June and met with Father Joset, Colonel Wright, Lieutenant Colonel Steptoe and a few other officers to discuss options for both peace and war. What was said is unknown but it is clear that while it was hoped for a peaceful solution war preparations needed to be made.

On July 4 Clarke, through one of his aides, issued the following order to Wright:

Brigadier General Clarke directs me to inform you that he has decided to place you in command of troops to be employed

---

[65] Burns, *The Jesuits*, 227

against the Indians north and east of Fort Walla-Walla. Six companies of the 3d regiment are now in march for Fort Walla-Walla, and from them and the present garrison of that post the column will be drawn.

The general's orders are as follows: that you proceed to Fort Walla-Walla, assume command of the troops; leave Brevet Lieutenant Colonel Steptoe a sufficient garrison to secure Walla-Walla.[66]

On August 7, 1858 Wright's force of nearly 600 men moved northwards while leaving Steptoe in command of a small garrison at Fort Walla Walla. The command crossed the Snake River and Fort Taylor was built, near present day Starbuck, Washington, as a supply depot for the expedition before continuing.

By late August the command received word that a large number of Indians were gathering in the area of Spokane Falls. Indians were observed, in the distance, but were chased off when Dragoons approached them. They also, on the 31st, attacked Wright's supply train but were driven off.

On September 1 Wright deployed his troops for battle as the Indians gathered in the woods and on the plain. Wright sent some of the troops towards the woods and the rest towards the plain, followed by the Dragoons. Indians attempted to rush the troops on the plain but suffered heavy losses by the new, long range rifles that Wright's troops were using.

Seeing the Indians confused the Dragoons rushed through the infantry line and towards the Indians causing the warriors to

---

[66] US Congress, *Annual Message, 1858*, 363

scatter and retreat. The battle had lasted less than four hours and Wright's command did not suffer a single loss.

After resting his command Wright marched northwards, on September 5, towards the Spokane River only to see another force of Indians in the distance. Wright stopped so that his supply train was not spread out and deployed his troops.

The Indians set fire to the grass between them and the soldiers. Wright ordered his troops through the flames and forcing the warriors to retreat. Whenever a large group of warriors were spotted they were subject to artillery barrage before the troops attacked.

Wright pushed the battle for twenty-five miles before calling an end. The losses for the Indians were again heavy, and they had lost two chiefs in the battle. After the battle the Indians were dismayed and their spirits were broken. They had enough of war.

On September 7, Wright headed towards Spokane Falls where Chief Garry came to plead for peace for the Spokanes. Wright listened to Garry and then replied:

> I have met you in two bloody battles; you have been badly whipped; you have lost several chiefs and many warriors, killed and wounded. I have not lost a man or animal; I have a large force, and you Spokanes, Coeur d' Alenes, Pelouses, and Pend d' Oreilles may unite, and I can defeat you as badly as before. I did not come into this country to ask you for peace; I came here to fight. Now, when you are tired of war, and ask for peace, I will tell you what you must do: You must come to me with your arms, with your women and children, and everything you have, and lay them at my feet; you must put your faith in me and trust to my mercy. If you do this, I shall then dictate the terms upon which I will grant

you peace. If you do not do this, war will be made on you this year and next, and until your nation shall be exterminated.[67]

The next day the command continued marching eastward and caught sight of a large group of Indian horses being herded southwards and out of range of the army. Wright ordered them captured and then was in a quandary of what to do with them.

Wright wanted, at first, to keep them but was concerned that the Indians would cause them to stampede along the march which would also cause a loss to the government horses as well. Wright appointed a board of officers to recommend what to do with the horses. It was decided to allow the officers and quartermaster to keep what was needed and the rest to be shot. However, many of the retained horses were still too wild for use and all were finally shot.

Father Joset sent Wright a message stating that the Indians knew they were defeated and had asked Joset to be their spokesman for peace. Wright responded by saying there would be a council of peace at the Mission of the Sacred Heart and all who participated in the war must come in with their guns, families and possessions.

Wright, and his command, reached the Mission on September 13 and on the 17th the council began. Many of the Indians admitted their guilt, expressed sorrow for the war and agreed to the demands of the government in a treaty that was signed by those who were there.

---

[67] Ibid, 393-394

For those who couldn't make the Mission council another council was scheduled for the Ned-Whauld River (Latah Creek) on September 23rd. Kamiakin came in the night before but left before Wright arrived for fear of being taken prisoner or worse. Kamiakin then fled to Canada.

The council at the Ned-Whauld River was similar to the one held at the Mission. Indians expressed their guilt and sorrow and signed the treaty Wright has prepared.

At the end of the day Yakama Chief Owhi rode into the council saying he also wanted peace. Colonel Wright reminded Owhi that Owhi had deceived Wright in 1856 by promising to bring in all his people but instead vanishing with them. Colonel Wright then told Owhi to send for his son, Yakama Chief Qualchan, and then placed Chief Owhi in chains.

A few days later Qualchan, unaware of the request, arrived at the council site. Wright recognized Qualchan and ordered him hung. Owhi was shot when he attempted to escape a few days later.

Wright also several other Indians to be hanged for their participation in the Yakama war.

Another minor council was held on September 30 when members of the Palouse tribe met with him on the Palouse River. Wright did not make a treaty with them but told them that war would fall upon them if they didn't stay in their own country. Wright also called for the surrender of those who had stolen Army cattle. Those that stepped forward were hanged at the council site before the Army continued towards Fort Walla Walla.

The command reached Fort Walla Walla on October 5 and the war was considered closed.

While Wright executed his operations in eastern Washington Major Robert Garnett lead around 300 soldiers, from Fort Simcoe, in operations in central Washington starting August 10. They did not have the success of Colonel Wright's forces and suffered only one loss- Lieutenant Jesse Allen who was killed by friendly fire in an early morning attack on an Indian camp. They returned back to Fort Simcoe on September 23.[68]

When they were camped 15 miles from Fort Simcoe Major Garnett sent a messenger to his wife saying that they would be back at the fort the next day. The messenger was immediately sent back to the returning troops and told Garnett the sad news that his wife had died about a week before.

1859-1860: A phony war

Because of the retreat of Lieutenant Colonel Edward Steptoe, Brigadier General William Harney was assigned, in June 1858, as the first commander of the newly established Department of Oregon. Harney's orders were to purse the Indians in the Columbia Plateau region until they were defeated. Harney arrived at Fort Vancouver on October 24 after learning of the success Colonel Wright.

---

[68] Ibid., 379-380

While peace was declared between the Indians and the Americans. Another issue was brewing because British and American governments were locked over the ownership of the San Juan Islands. This was caused by the interpretation of the Treaty of Washington signed in 1846 which set the northern boundary of the United States and then *to the middle of the channel which separates the continent of Vancouver's Island, and thence southerly through the middle of said channel...* The treaty recognized only one channel that passed through the San Juan Islands. However, there are really two channels and depending on which channel one interprets the treaty as meaning gave the Islands to either country.[69]

The Islands were first claimed by the Hudson's Bay Company (HBC) and was used for raising sheep. The Americans living there said that HBC was on American soil must pay taxes for the sheep. HBC official protested when several sheep were seized and sold.

On June 15, 1859 an HBC boar was found tearing up a garden tended by one of the Americans living there. The American, who had protested the HBC's boars knocking down his fence and eating his garden, took out his gun and shot the boar dead. The incident known as The Pig War has just begun.

On July 9 Harney paid a courtesy call to Sir James Douglas, Governor of Vancouver's Island, where he learned about the shooting of the pig. Harney then went to the San Juan's and

---

[69] Keith Murray, *The Pig War*, 23

told the Americans to make a petition requesting military protection against Indians raids.

Several days later, Harney ordered Captain George Pickett to take his company from Fort Bellingham to the Islands and build a fort to protect the Americans against Indian raids. Pickett was also ordered to prevent the arrest of any American by the British government.

Pickett landed on July 27 and issued a proclamation stating that *this being United States Territory, no laws, other than those of the United States, nor courts, except such as are held by virtue of said laws, will be recognized or allowed on this island.*[70] The British responded by sending two warships with orders to land their marines and drive the Americans off the island if they didn't immediately withdraw.

Being alarmed at this, Pickett wrote to Lieutenant Colonel Silas Casey about the situation. Upon receiving the message Lieutenant Colonel Casey thought there was a possibility for action and sent Major Granville Haller (now commanding Fort Townsend), and his company, to the Island.

(At the height of the incident the Americans had 461 men facing the British which had five warships and 2140 men.)

Many people, on both sides, thought it was exciting that the United States and Great Britain were about to go to war. British citizens from Victoria went to the San Juan Island and were disappointed that there was a lack of overt hostilities. They also

---

[70] George Adams, *General William S. Harney:Prince of Dragoons*, 199

notices that British officers were in the American camp talking with Captain Pickett and his officers.

The US newspaper *The Pioneer and Democrat* summed up the feelings of most Americans when it reported: *HMS* Tribune, *lies with spring cables and her guns double-shotted broadsides to the camp of Capt. Pickett; her decks are covered with readcoats, having onboard 450 marines and some 180 sappers and miners. We thank God we have, in this officer of the Department of Oregon, a man equal to any and all emergencies in the protection of American citizens in the Northwest Coast.*[71]

On September 3, the British ambassador, in Washington DC, received a letter from Governor Douglas about the killing of the boar and the landing of US troops. With letter in hand the ambassador went to the US Secretary of State and was assured that Harney acted on his own and without orders the government.

The British reaction to the denial of any knowledge of Harney's action was harsh. It stated that *it is of the nature of US citizens to push themselves where they had no right to go, and it is the nature of the US government not to venture to disavow acts which they cannot have face to approve.*[72]

Since the crisis had been started by the military, President James Buchanan thought, it should be settled by the military. He then ordered General Scott to travel to Washington Territory and put Harney in check. Scott arrived at Fort Vancouver on October 20.

---

[71] Al Cummings, *San Juan: The Powder-keg Island*, 48
[72] Murray, *Pig War*, 54

Scott met with both Harney and Picket and was informed of the situation. Harney then protested Scott for being there.

Arriving at Fort Townsend, on October 25, Scott started a series of correspondence with Douglas. It was agreed that both sides should withdraw all troops except for 100 men, from each side, to maintain order and to protect against Indian raids.

Pickett returned back to Fort Bellingham and Captain Lewis Hunt was put in charge. Seeing that all was in order Scott then returned to Washington DC to report the incident.

When Harney knew General Scott was back in Washington DC he ordered Hunt, and his company, off the Island and back to Fort Steilcoom. He then ordered Pickett, and company, back to the Island and turn them over to the Whatcom County government.

When President Buchanan heard of this he ordered that Harney be relieved of command. Colonel George Wright assumed command of the Department of Oregon on July 5, 1860.[73]

The war was over.

While the war was over the dispute wasn't. Because of world events it wasn't until November 20, 1868 that the American and British governments agreed to let the King of Prussia decide who owned the Islands. On October 21, 1871 the German decision was published and on November 8 the British issued orders to get their troops off of American territory.[74]

---

[73] Carl Schlicke, *General George Wright: Guardian of the Pacific Coast*, 205
[74] Murray, *Pig War*, 74

1861-1889: Return to Stability

Following the end of the Pig War brought several changes to the Indians and whites who occupied the land. The first was the closing down of all Hudson's Bay Company posts south of the 49th parallel; this included their post at Fort Vancouver.

The next was the establishment annual deployment (starting in 1859) of dragoons, from Fort Walla Walla, to the Snake River to protect immigrants from the Shoshoni and Bannock Indians. These patrols continued until the Indians turned away from attacking the wagon trains that were passing through their territory.

When the Civil War came many southern officers and soldiers resigned their commission or deserted their posts in order to join the armies of their states. Also, most of the regular units, still loyal to the Union, were recalled back east and their duties were taken over by volunteers.

The duties of the volunteers were the same ones as the regular forces before they left. Under the command of Brigadier General George Wright, commander of the Department of the Pacific, and Brigadier General Benjamin Alvord, commander of the Department of Oregon, the units were to protect the settlers and Indians from each other. The units were also told to maintain order and to protect the Territory from Confederate sympathizers.

After the Civil War volunteers were mustered out and regular units began to arrive in the Territory to pick up their duties once again.

It is interesting to note that after the Wright-Garnett expedition of 1858 there were no Indian wars in Washington Territory. However, there were many of them that occurred in both Oregon State and Idaho Territory after that date. Peace had come to the seized lands for both the victor and the defeated.

Guide to the Sites and Personnel of the Washington Territory Indian Wars

This section is intended to be used as a reference guide to the locations of historic sites and personalities of the Washington wars of the 1850s and 1860s. Many of these locations are marked by monuments and interpretive signs today. Other site locations are unknown and the best location estimate is given. Individual ranks, and titles, are given at the highest level they used while assigned to Washington Territory. Dates of duties and actions are approximate due to missing or conflicting information. Symbols following the site or person indicate the following:

B - Historical building(s) and/or reconstruction

D- A building or member not owned and/or subject to a specific Catholic religious order

HBC-Hudson's Bay Company post

I - Interpretive center or museum

M - Monument or interpretive sign

NPS - National Park or Historic site and operated by the National Park Service

NWC- Northwest Company post

OMI- A building or member belonging and/or subject to the Oblates of Mary Immaculate

PFC- Pacific Fur Company post

SJ- A building or member belonging and/or subject to the Society of Jesus (Jesuits)

SP – City, County or State Park

USA-United States Army soldier or post

USN-United States Navy

X - No marker indicating location and/or historical importance

? –Information is unknown or uncertain

Note: The areas surrounding many of the markers are on private property. While many of these markers are on public lands there maybe a cost involved to see them.

Locations of battles and places by county

Washington

Astoin County
Chief Timothy State Park (M,SP)

Clark County
Vancouver, Camp (USA,I,M,B,NPS)
Vancouver, Fort (HBC,NPS,B)

Cowlitz County
Monticello (M)

Columbia County
Taylor, Fort (X)

Douglas County
Chelan, Camp (X)

Grays Harbor County
Chehalis, Camp (X)

Island County
Ebey's Landing (NPS,B,M,I)

Jefferson County
Mason, Fort (X)

Klickitat County
Andrew Bolon markers (M)
Eel Trail (X)

King County
Alder, Fort (X)
Henderson, Fort (X)
Decatur, Fort (M)
Dent, Fort (X)
Duwamish, Fort (X)
Lander, Fort (X)
Muckleshoot Prairie, Battle of (X)
Muckleshoot Prairie, Camp (X)
Thomas, Fort (X)
Tilton, Fort (X)

Kittitas County
Immaculate Conception Mission (OMI,X)
Yakima River Battlefield (X)

Kitsap County
Kitsap, Fort (X)
Malikoff, Fort (X)
Point No Point Treaty Grounds (M)
Port Gamble Cemetery (M)
Townsend, Fort (USA,M,SP)

Lewis County

Arkansas, Fort (X)
Borst, Fort (B)
Cowlitz, Fort(HBC,USA,X)
Saint Francis Xaiver Mission (D,M,B)

Okanogan County
Caribou Trail (M)
McLoughlin Canyon, Battle of (M)
Okanogan, Fort (HBC,SP)

Pacific County
Cape Disappointment, Fort (USA,B,I,SP)

Pierce County
Brannon's Prairie, Battle of (M)
Connell's Prairie, Battle of (M)
Eaton, Fort (M)
Hays, Fort(X)
Hicks, Fort (X)
Leschi's Grave (M)
Leschi Hanging site (M)
Maloney, Fort (M)
McAllister (X)
Naches Pass (X)
Nisqually, Fort (HBC,B,I,M)

Pike, Fort (X)
Preston, Fort(X)
Posey, Fort (X)
Raglan, Fort (X)
Sales, Fort (X)
Steilacoom, Fort (USA,B,I,M)
Stevens,Fort (X)
White, Fort (X)
White River, Battle of (X)

San Juan Island County
American Camp (USA, NPS, B)

Skamania County
Cascades, Fort (M)
Cascades of the Columbia, Battle of (M)
Gilliam, Fort (X)

Snohomish County
Ebey, Fort (X)
Point Elliot Treaty (M)

Spokane County
Colville-Walla Walla Road (M)
Drumheller Springs (M,SP)
Four Lakes, Battle of (M)
Four Lakes, Camp (X)

Hanging Tree Site (M)
Horse Slaughter Site (M)
Plante's Ferry (M,SP)
Mullan Road (M)
Ned-Whauld River, Camp on the (X)
Spokane, Fort (NPS,B)
Garry's Grave (M)
Spokane House (M,B,I,SP)
Spokane Plains, Battle of (M,SP)
Washington, Camp (M)

Stevens County
Colvile, Fort (HBC,M,SP)
Colville, Fort (USA,M)
Saint Paul's Mission (SJ,M,B,SP)
Tshimakain Mission Site (M)

Thurston County
Henness, Fort (M)
Medicine Creek Treaty Grounds (M)
Miller, Fort (X)
Olympia (X)

Walla Walla County
Bennett, Fort (X)
Frenchtown, Battle of (M)

Mason, Fort (X)
Nez Percés, Fort (HBC,M)
Saint Rose Mission (OMI,M)
Walla Walla Council Grounds (M)
Walla Walla, Fort (USA,B,I,M)
Waters, Fort (X)
Whitman Mission (NPS,I,M)

Whatcom County
Bellingham, Fort (B)

Whitman County
Tohotomine, Battle of (M,SP)

Yakima County
Edgar Rock (M)
Eel Trail (X)
Holy Cross Mission (OMI,X)
Kamiakin's Garden (X)
Naches Pass (X)
Nechess River, Camp (USA,M)
Saint Joseph's Mission (OMI,M,B)
Satus Creek, Battle of (M)
Simcoe, Fort (USA,B,I,SP)

Toppenish Creek, Battle of (X)

Two Buttes, Battle of (M)

Yakama Valley (X)

Oregon
Clatsop County
Clatsop, Fort (USA,NPS,B,M)
Umatilla County
Henrietta, Fort (B,I,SP)
Wallowa County
Grande Ronde, Battle of (X)
Wasco County
Dalles, Fort (USA,M,B)

Idaho
Canyon County
Boise, Fort (HBC,B,M,SP)
Ward Massacre Site (M,SP)
Kootenai County
Mission of the Sacred Heart
Nez Perce County
Lapwai Mission

Alden, Fort (X) (1856) Blockhouse. Named after Captain James Alden. A temporary blockhouse built by the Northern Battalion of the Second Volunteer Regiment. Location: King County. Sited sixty feet south of the Snoqualmie River and short distant above Snoqualmie Falls.

Alvord, Brigadier General Benjamin USA (1813-1884) Fourth Infantry Regiment. Second Seminole Indian and Mexican Wars. Chief Paymaster for the District of Oregon(1854-1860); Promoted to Brigadier-General in the volunteers (1862). During the Civil War he was Commander, District of Oregon (1862-1865).

Archer, Captain James USA (1817-1864) Ninth Infantry Regiment. Mexican War. Yakama Valley campaign (spring 1856); Garnett expedition (Fall 1858); commanded Fort Simcoe (1858-1859). Service with Confederate forces in the Civil War.

Arkansas, Fort (X) (1855) Blockhouse. Built by settlers. Location: Lewis County. Sited along the Cowlitz River near Castle Rock at the southeast end of Arkansas Valley.

American Camp (USA, NPS, B) (1859-1874) This was the American quarters during the dispute over the San Juan Islands and established near the HBC's Belle Vue Farm. Location: San Juan County. Location: San Juan County. Located on the south end of

San Juan Island. Also known as Camp Picket, Post of San Juan, Camp Fred Steele and Camp San Juan Island.

Augur, Captain Christopher USA (1821-1898) Fourth Infantry Regiment. Mexican War. Rains expedition (November 1855). Service with Union forces during the Civil War.

Basket Fort See Nechess River, Camp

Bellingham, Fort (USA, B) (1856-1860) One of two post to protect the Whatcom coal mining district from Indian attacks. The first was a small blockhouse erected in 1855. The second one was built, under the direction of Captain George Pickett in response to petitions of settlers. Only one officer quarters remain. Location: Whatcom County. Quarters are located on Bancroft Street, north of downtown Bellingham.

Bennan's Praire See Brannon's Prairie

Bennett, Fort (X) (1855-1856) Named for Captain Charles Bennett who was killed in action. A temporary post built by Oregon Volunteers for winter quarters. Location: Walla Walla County. Sited two miles east of the Whitman Mission along the north bank of the Walla Walla River.

Blanchet, Archbishop François D (1795-1883) Appointed Vicar-General of the Oregon Country (1837); Arrived in Oregon

Country (1838); Consecrated Bishop (1845); Named Archbishop of Oregon City (1846).

Blockhouses These are fortified structures constructed with openings for shooting weapons. During the early stages of the Yakama War settlers were urged to build blockhouses for protection and not to abandoned their homes and property. Nearly fifty temporary blockhouses were constructed, most of them in the Puget Sound area around rivers or prairies. Settlers erected thirty-three, militia erected thirty-five and regulars erected seven blockhouses. These structures were sometimes referred to as forts. See individual listings for location.

Bolon, Andrew J. (1826?-1855). Elected Clark County Sheriff (1850-1851); Served in territorial legislature (1854); Sub-Indian Agent for the Yakama tribe (1855).

Bolon, Andrew J. markers (M) The murder of Indian Agent Andrew J. Bolon in September 1855, was one of the major events that triggered the Yakama War. Location: Klickitat County. A marker on a county road, 5 miles northeast of Goldendale, is substantially south of the actual site on the old Eel Trail between Celilo Falls and the Yakima Valley. A second marker is at the actual site at Wahk-shum spring. The first marker is located at the intersection of Cedar Valley and Monument Road, the location of the first monument. The second marker at Wahk-Shum spring is approximately 4.5 miles north on Monument Road.

Boise, Fort (HBC,B, M,SP) July 15, 1855. Major Granville Haller was ordered back to the Ward Massacre site and to find and punish the Indians responsible. He took 150 men with him and arrived at Fort Boise where a council was held with the Indians. During the talks it was noted that four of the participants of the Ward killing were among the present. Haller ordered them arrested and tried before a military commission which found them guilty. One of the Indians was shot while trying to escape but the other three were marched to the Ward site. Here gallows were built and they were hanged. Location: Canyon County, Idaho. Original location of Fort Boise is on the Snake River, west of Parma, on the Old Fort Boise Road, and in the Fort Boise Wildlife Management Area. A replica of Fort Boise is located in Parma.

Borst, Fort (B) (1855-1856) Blockhouse. This was built in 1856 to guard a river crossing on the Skookemchuck River. The fort was later designated as a supply depot by the Washington Volunteers. Location: Lewis County. It has been moved to Fort Borst Park in Centralia.

Brannon's Prairie, Battle of (M) December 4, 1855. The command of Lieutenant William Slaughter was encamped on Brannon's Prairie. On December 4, in heavy fog, Chief Kanaskat and his band of Klickitat warriors surrounded the camp, fired a volley and then withdrew into the darkness. Two markers commemorate the Indian attack on the settlers' homes on October

28, 1855 and the location where Lieutenant Slaughter was killed. Location: Pierce County. The park is along the old Kent-Auburn Hwy at the junction of 30th Street NE and Auburn Way N. Also known as Bennan's Prairie.

Caribou Trail (M) This was one of the main routes into the gold fields of Canada. It was also a main travel route for Indians and fur trappers as well as a cattle trail. Location: Okanogan County. Sign describing travel in the Okanogan Valley is three miles south of Okanogan on Highway 97.

Cataldo Mission See Mission of the Sacred Heart

Camp at the Cabins See Gilliam, Fort

Canby, Fort See Cape Disappointment, Fort

Cape Disappointment, Fort (USA, B, I, SP) (1862-1950) Built by USA for the defense of the Columbia River. The quarters for officers and men were located along the shores of Baker Bay. Very little remains of the pre-1890s fort. Location: Pacific County. Located in Cape Disappointment State Park. Also called Fort Canby.

Casey, Lieutenant Colonel Silas USA (1807-1882) Ninth Infantry Regiment. Second Seminole Indian and Mexican wars.

Commander, Puget Sound District (1856-1861). Service with Union forces in the Civil War.

Cascades of the Columbia, Battle of (M) March 26-28, 1856. As units of the Ninth Infantry moved westwards to join other units for a Spring campaign against the Indians, various bands of Yakamas, Chinooks and Klickitats moved eastward and attack the undermanned blockhouses at Fort Cascades. When word of this attack reached Fort Vancouver, Lieutenant Philip Sheridan took forty men upriver on a steamboat and fought their way to the besieged blockhouses. At Fort Dallas, Lieutenant Colonel Edward Steptoe took 200 men downriver and fought their way to the blockhouses. Faced with a superior force the Indians scattered and were pursued by US forces; several were caught and made prisoners. When Colonel George Wright arrived a military commissioned was formed and the prisoners were found guilty of the attack. Eight Indians were hanged including Chief Chenowith.

Cascades, Fort (M) (1855-1861) Blockhouse. A group of three blockhouses built by USA troops to protect the portage road around the Cascade Rapids on the Columbia River. The first blockhouse was built at the foot of the rapids and is known as the Lower Blockhouse. The second was about five miles upriver and is known as the Upper Blockhouse (also called Fort Lugenbeel). The third blockhouse was located about half way between the two and was known as the Middle Blockhouse (also called Fort Rains).

Location: Skamania County. Located between North Bonneville and the Bonneville Dam.

Cataldo Mission See Mission of the Sacred Heart

Chehalis, Camp (X) (1860-1861) Built by USA troops to protect settlers in the area. Location: Grays Harbor County. Sited near the mouth of the Chehalis River. Also called Fort Chehalis but never officially designated a fort.

Chehalis, Fort See Chehalis, Camp

Chelan, Camp (X) (1879-1880). A temporary post to watch over the local Indian population. Due to its remote location the post was abandoned and transferred to Camp Spokane. Location: Douglas County. Located along Foster Creek, near Bridgeport.

Chenowith Cascades Tribe (?-1856). One of the leaders during the Battle of Cascades of the Columbia (1856); captured during the battle, tried and hanged (1856). Also spelled Chenowuth and Chenoweth.

Chief Timothy State Park (M, SP) A large park is at the site of Nez Pérces Chief Timothy's winter home, near where the Steptoe expedition crossed the Snake in 1858. Location: Astoin County. The park is about 7 miles west of Clarkston on U.S. Hwy 12.

Chirouse, Father Casimir (1821-1892) OMI. Was one of the first Catholics to be ordained in Oregon Country (Father Charles Pandosy was ordained at the same time) (1848); Worked among the Yakama and Kittitas tribes (1848-1856); Worked among the tribes in the Puget Sound region (1856-1878); Administered the Sacrament of Extreme Unction (last rites) to Chief Seattle (1866); He also composed a Snohomish-English/English-Snohomish dictionary.

Clatsop, Fort (NPS, B, M) (1805-1806). This was the first USA post in the Pacific Northwest. It was constructed to increase American claims on the Pacific Northwest. Location: Clatsop County, Oregon. Located in the Fort Clatsop National Memorial near Astoria.

Collins, Fort (X) (1855) Blockhouse. Built by Volunteers. Location: Mason County. Sited near Hungerford Point in the southeast section of the county.

Columbia Barracks See Vancouver, Camp

Colville, Camp See Colville, Fort

Colvile, Fort (HBC, M, SP) (1826-1871). This was the regional headquarters for HBC after Spokane House was abandoned. The original spelling of the post was later altered by the Americans. The site of the HBC post is now under the waters of Lake Roosevelt. The first gold rush in Washington Territory occurred near here in 1855. Location: Stevens County. A marker is located in St. Paul's Mission State Park. The park is located 3 miles west of Kettle Falls on Highway 395. .

Colville, Fort (USA, M) (1859-1882). Built on the east side of Mill Creek, near the present day city of Colville, after the local gold rush had started and to control the Indians of the region. Location: Stevens County. A marker exists at the site on the north side of State Highway 20, one mile east on Highway 20 and 2 miles north on Aladdin Road. Also known as Harney's Depot and Camp Colville.

Colville-Walla Walla Road (M). A trail originally used by Spokane Indians to move between the Snake (near Walla Walla) and Colville Rivers. Location: Spokane County. On Highway 2 near Coulee-Hite Road.

Connell's Prairie, Battle of (M) March 4, 1856. Most of the battles of this theater were fought within a ten-mile radius of this area and was the last large scale battle west of the Cascades. Two companies of Washington Volunteers were ordered to establish a ferry and blockhouse at the White River Crossing at Connell's Prairie. About 150 Klickitat Indians, under the leadership of the Nisqually Chief Leschi, attacked them. The volunteers counter attacked and drove the Indians off the battlefield. The Indian defeat here shattered the Indian alliance in the western half of the territory. Location: Pierce County. A marker is located near Lake

Tapps at the intersection of Connells Prairie Road and Barkubine Road East.

Connell's Prairie Blockhouse See Hays, Fort

Cowlitz, Fort (HBC, USA, X) (1837-1860?). A small HBC post. Also known as Cowlitz Farm. Later the USA established a fort in the same area called Fort at Cowlitz Landing. Location: Lewis County. Sited along the Cowlitz River near Toledo.

Dalles, Fort (USA, M, B) (1850-1867). This was the principal military fort for the interior region of Washington Territory and Oregon. It was built over the former Methodist Wascopam Mission, along the Columbia River. During the early Yakama Wars it served as operational headquarters for the Army. Location: Wasco County, Oregon. Located in The Dalles. Also known as Camp Drum.

Davidson, Lieutenant Henry USA (1831-1899) First Dragoons. Mexican War. Wright expedition (Fall 1858). Served with Confederate forces in the Civil War.

Decatur, Fort (M) (1855) Blockhouse. A two-gun blockhouse built by Marines from the *USS Decatur* and used during the Indian attack on Seattle. Location: King County. Bronze tablet near the corner of Occidental and South Main in downtown Seattle.

Dent, Fort (X) (1855) Blockhouse. Named after Captain Fredrick Dent. Built by US Army troops at the confluence of the Black and White Rivers. Location: King County. Sited in Fort Dent Park in Tukwila.

Drum, Camp See Dalles, Fort

Drumheller Springs (M, SP) This was the site of the first school in Oregon Territory, established by Spokane Chief Garry, in 1830. This was also the only freshwater spring for travelers between Spokane and the confluence of the Spokane and Columbia rivers in the early 1800s. Location: Spokane County. Located on Ash Street near Fairview Avenue in Spokane.

Duwamish, Fort (X) (1855) Blockhouse. Luther Collins donated one acre of land to build a blockhouse so that the settler could have protection in case of an attack. Location: King County. West of the Georgetown Steam plant Museum (6605 13th Avenue South) in Seattle.

Eaton, Fort (M) (1855) Blockhouse. It was built on the Eaton Donation Land Claim by settlers for protection from Indians. Location: Pierce County. South of Lacy off of State Highway 510

Ebey, Fort (X) (1855) Blockhouse. Named after United States Customs collector, Isaac Ebey. Built by Washington Volunteers who later transferred to Fort Alden. Location: Snohomish County. Near Everett on Ebey Island about one mile upstream from Lowell.

Ebey's Landing (B, M, NPS, I) Two historic blockhouses (called James Davis and John Crockett Blockhouses) from the 1850s as well as the site of the Isaac Ebey homestead, who was beheaded by Haida warriors in 1857, are in the area. Location: Island County. Follow Highway 20 from Anacortes or Highway 525 from the Mukilteo ferry crossing.

Edgar Rock (M) Named after John Edgar who learned from his Yakama wife that Chief Kamiakin was planning to attack the column of Lieutenant William Slaughter. Edgar managed to warn Slaughter near the rock that bears his name. However, when the Indians learned of this they killed Edgar when he returned to his home. Location: Yakima County. Along Highway 410 southeast of Cliffdell.

Eel Trail (X). A north-south route used by Indians and whites that went from the area around Celilo Falls, near The Dalles, into Yakama country. Location: Yakima & Klickitat Counties.

English, Lieutenant Colonel Thomas USA (1827-1876) Ninth Infantry Regiment. Commanded US forces on San Juan Island (1861); Promoted to Lieutenant Colonel of the volunteers (1861); commanded First Washington Territory Infantry (1862 &

1864); Acting Assistant Provost-Marshall-General for the State of Oregon and Territory of Washington (1863-1865).

Four Lakes, Battle of (M) September 1, 1858. On August 31, Colonel George Wright led 600 men onto the Spokane Plains and noticed Indians maintaining their distance from the troops. Indians tried to set the Plains on fire but were unsuccessful. The next day Wright ordered his troops to attack the gathering of Indians that blocked their way. Wright's command had new rifles and were able to shoot long distances without fear of retaliation. Wright's Dragoons charged the Indians and attacked them with sabers and pistols before the Indians broke and retreated. The Dragoons gave chase for about one mile before giving up. Wright's command suffered no casualties. Location: Spokane County. A monument in Four Lakes commemorates the fight at the north end of Electric Avenue, just south of the freeway. Note: The Heritage Markers that point towards the location of the marker were installed by the Washington State Department of Transportation at the request of the author.

Four Lakes, Camp (X) Colonel George Wright's command rested, on September 2, 1858, around the south-east section of Silver Lake, located near Four Lake. Here Colonel Wright wrote his report about the battle that had occurred the day before. Location: Spokane County.

Fred Steele, Camp See American Camp

Frenchtown, Battle of (M) December 7-10, 1855. Lieutenant Colonel James Kelly's Oregon Volunteers left Fort Dallas in early December heading towards Fort Walla Walla (HBC). Near the confluence of the Touchet and Walla Walla Rivers Kelly meet with PeoPeoMoxMox but the meeting did not go well. Suspecting deceit, Kelly took PeoPeoMoxMox and several other Indians as hostage. Advancing towards the old Whitman Mission the Volunteers found their way blocked by a line of Indians. The next morning Kelly was able to move his command into a better position to repulse several attacks on their position. On the third day the Volunteers attacked several key Indian positions which caused the Indians to retreat. Location: Walla Walla County. One mile west of the Whitman Mission NHS on Highway 12. Also called Battle of Waiilatpu.

Gansevoort, Captain Guert USN (1812-1868) Mexican War. Commanded *USS Decatur*. Served with Union forces in the Civil War.

Garnett, Major Robert USA (1819-1861) Ninth Infantry Regiment. Mexican War. Commanded Fort Simcoe (1856-1858); commanded Garnett expedition (Fall 1858). Served with Confederate forces in the Civil War.

Garry (1811?-1892) Spokane Tribe. Met with Governor Isaac Steven's at tribal council at Anotine Plante's cabin (1855); Urged members of the tribe not to take part in the Yakama War when it started (1855); Met with Lieutenant Colonel Steptoe and asked where Steptoe was going with a large force (May 1858); Failed to prevent members of his tribe from joining the latter half of the Yakama War. Signed peace treaty with Colonel George Wright (September 1858)

Garry's Grave (M) The grave of this influential Spokane Indian chief is in Greenwood Cemetery, 211 N Government Way, Spokane.

Gilliam, Fort (X) (1848) Named for Colonel Cornelius Gilliam. A supply depot and a base of operations built by Oregon Volunteers on the right side of the Columbia River. The post consisted of a few cabins and was often referred to as 'the Cabins'. Location: Skamania County. Near the Bonneville Dam, not far from Fort Cascade. Also called Camp at the Cabins.

Grande Ronde, Battle of (X) July 18, 1856. Frustrated with the military's attempts to remove Indians for white settlements, Governor Isaac Stevens planned a summer campaign into Walla Walla and Yakama Country. In early July a force of 400 volunteers, under the command of Lieutenant Colonel Benjamin Shaw marched into Oregon. In the Grande Ronde Valley, between the Blue and Wallowa Mountains, they encountered 300 Indians and attacked them. The Indians scattered and many were killed on the banks of the Grande Ronde River. The volunteers captured

Indian supplies and 200 horses. The horses were shot. Location: Wallowa County, Oregon.

Grant, Lieutenant Ulysses USA (1822-1885) Fourth Infantry Regiment. Mexican War. Quartermaster at Fort Vancouver (winter 1852-1853) Service with Union forces during the Civil War.

Gregg, Lieutenant David USA (1833-1916) First Dragoons. Battle of Tohotomine (May 1858). Service with Union forces during Civil War.

Hale, Calvin (1818-1887) Attended the Monticello Convention (1852); Served in territorial legislature (1854); Duty as Superintendent of Indian Affairs for both Washington and Idaho Territories (1862-1864).

Haller, Major Granville USA (1819-1897) Fourth Infantry Regiment. Second Seminole Indian and Mexican Wars. Commanded, Fort Dalles (1855-1856); Commanded expeditions against Indians of the Ward Massacre (summers 1854 & 1855); Battle of Toppenish Creek (October 1855); Rains expedition (November 1855); Yakama Valley campaign (Spring 1856); Commanded, Fort Townsend (Fall 1856-1859); San Juan Island Dispute (1859). Service with Union forces during the Civil War.

Hanging Tree Site (M) The area where tribal leader Qualchan and others were hanged during the September 1858 treaty council with Colonel George Wright. Location: Spokane County. A marking showing the location of the hanging tree is about four miles east of Spangle on the North Kentucky Trails Road.

Hangman Creek, Camp at See Ned-Whauld River, Camp on the

Harney, General William USA.(1800-1889) Second Seminole and Mexican wars; action against the Sioux Indians. Commander, Department of Oregon (1858-1860). Served with Union forces during the Civil War.

Harney's Depot See Colville, Fort.

Hays, Fort (X) (1856) Blockhouse. Named for Major Gilmore Hays, Second Reigment. Built by the central battalion of Washington Volunteers overlooking Connell's Prairie. Location: Pierce County. Sited near the town of Bonney Lake. Also called Connell's Prairie Blockhouse.

Henderson, Fort (X) (185?)Blockhouse. Built by the Northern Battalion of the Washington Volunteers from Fort Tilton. Location: King County. Sited on the Snoqualmie River, near the mouth of Patterson Creek, below Fall City. Also called Fort Patterson.

Henness, Fort (M) (1855-1856) Blockhouse. Named for Captain Benjamin Henness. It was built with a large stockade with two blockhouses and included several cabins. Washington

Volunteers often used it as well as local families used it for safety. Location: Thurston County. Rochester Grand Mound area, across from the Grand Mound Cemetery and south of Scatter Creek.

Henrietta, Fort (B, I, SP) (1855) Blockhouse. Named after Major Granville Haller's wife, Henrietta. Built by Oregon Volunteers. Used by Oregon Volunteers as a base of operations against tribes in the Walla Walla region. Location: Umatilla County, Oregon. Located at Fort Henrietta Park in Echo.

Hicks, Fort (X) (1855-1856) Blockhouse. Built by Washington Volunteers. Location: Pierce County. Sited between Fort Steilacoom and Puyallup near Spanaway Lake.

Holy Cross Mission (OMI, X) This mission was burned by US forces soon after the destruction of Saint Joseph's Mission. Location: Yakima County. Sited in the Lower Ahtanum Valley

Horse Slaughter Site (M) September 8-?, 1858 A few days after the Battle of Spokane Plains Colonel Wright's Dragoons captured over 800 Indian horses. It was decided that most should be killed and the rest used by the quartermaster. However, all were eventually killed due to their wild behavior. Location: Spokane County. The monument is located next to the recreational trail along the Spokane River about 1 mile west of the Interstate 90 rest stop near the I-90 Spokane River Bridge, 19 miles east of Spokane. Note: Disregard the inscription at the bottom of the marker saying monument moved one mile east of original location. It has been moved back to its original location.

Hunt, Captain Lewis USA. (1824-1886) 4th Infantry Regiment. Mexican War. San Juan Island Dispute (1859); Commanded US garrison on San Juan Island (1859). Served with Union forces in the Civil War.

Immaculate Conception Mission (OMI, X) After the burning of St. Joseph's Mission Volunteers rode to this mission, plundered it and then set it on fire sometime in November 1855. Location: Kittitas County. Sited close to the Manastash Creek near Ellensburg.

Kamiakin (1800-1877) Yakama Tribe. Donated land so that St. Joseph's Mission could be built (1852); Oversaw a council, of various tribes, in the Grande Ronde Valley to discuss how to keep whites off their lands; after the Walla Walla Council of 1855 he formed an alliance of 14 tribes to wage war against the whites(1855); leader of Indian forces in the Battle of Toppenish (October 1855); Wounded at the Battle of Four Lakes (September 1858).

Kamiakin's Garden (X) One of the first irrigation projects in the Territory was located here. Here Kamiakin grew vegetables that he shared with his family, tribe and the priests at Saint Joseph's Mission. Location: Yakima County. Sited west of Union Gap near the intersection of Slavin and Lower Ahtanum Roads.

Kanaskat (?-1856) Klikitat Tribe. The Chief who lead the attack on Lieutenant Slaughter's command at Brannon's Prairie. He was captured by the forces under the command of Captain Erasmus Keys during the Battle of Lemmon's Prairie. Kanaskat was shot in the back while soldiers were detaining him. While he still struggled another soldier placed his musket on Kanaskat's temple and killed him. With the death of Kanaskat the Puget Sound tribes lost another voice in the war against the whites.

Keyes, Captain Erasmus USA (1810-1895) Third Artillery. Battle of Lemmon's Prairie (1856); Wright campaign (Fall 1858). Served with Union forces during the Civil War.

Kitsap, Fort (X) (1855) Blockhouse. Named for friendly Yakama Chief Kitsap. Built by Washington Volunteers. Location: Kitsap County. Port Madison on Bainbridge Island.

Lander, Fort (X) (1856) Blockhouse. Named after Captain Edward Lander, Second Regiment. Originally built by Second Regiment Washington Volunteers and later moved upriver on the south bank of the Duwamish River and enclosed with a stockade. Location: King County. Sited on the Duwamish River, north of Boeing Field.

Lapwai Mission (I, M, NP) The site of Henry and Eliza Spalding's (also spelled Spaulding) mission among the Nez Percés was the first white home in present day Idaho. The Mission was closed down after the attack on the Whitmans. Location: Nez Perce

County, Idaho. Located at the Nez Percé National Historical Park ten miles east of Lewiston on Highway 95.

Latah Creek, Camp at See Ned-Whauld River, Camp on the

Lemmon's Prairie, Battle of (X) March 1, 1856. 200 warriors attacked the camp of Lieutenant August Kautz, Fourth US Infantry, near the site where Lieutenant Slaughter was killed. Kautz sent for help and Captain Erasmus Keyes arrived with his company of Third Artillery. The combined US forces attacked the Indians forcing them to scatter and retreat. Location: King County. Sited near Enumclaw. Also called Battle of Muckleshoot Prairie.

Leschi (1808-1858) Nisqually Tribe. Leschi traveled to Olympia to protest the terms of the Medicine Creek Treaty. Acting Governor Charles Mason ordered Leschi and his brother, Quiemuth, to be taken into protective custody (1855); Lead attack against Connell's Prairie (March 1856);Taken into custody and his brother turned himself in (November 1856). Quiemuth was killed in Governor Isaac Steven's office (November 1856); Tried (twice), convicted and hanged for the murder of Abram Moses (1858).

Leschi's Grave (M) Leschi's remains now rest in the Pullayup Indian Reservation Cemetery, which is next to the junction of Interstate 5 and State Hwy 167 in Tacoma.

Leschi's Hanging Site (M) The Nisqually chief and nominal leader of the Puget Sound hostiles was hanged at the northern end of Lake Steilacoom on February 19, 1858. Location: Pierce County. A small monument commemorates the event in a shopping center parking lot at 8107 Steilacoom Boulevard SW in Lakewood and near Fort Steilacoom.

Lugenbeel, Fort See Cascades, Fort

Malikoff, Fort (X) (1853-?) A small fort designed to protect the settlers from attacks. Location: Kitsap County. Sited around Port Gamble.

Maloney, Fort (M) (1855-1856) Blockhouse. Named after Captain Maurice Maloney, Fourth US Infantry. Location: Pierce County. North of the bridge over the Pullayup River near Meridian Street. Lemmons Prairie was the site of several skirmishes during the war.

Mashel Massacre (X, SP) March 31, 1856. In a series of patrols around the Nisqually and Mashel Rivers area Volunteers, under the command of Captain Hamilton Maxon, attack Indian settlements of mostly unarmed women, children and old men as they tried to hid themselves in the forest. Location: Pierce County. Sited at the Nisqually-Mashel State Park on State Highway 7 near Eatonville. Also known as Maxon Masscare.

Mason, Fort (X) (1855-1856) Blockhouse. Named after Charles Mason, Secretary of Washington Territory and Acting Governor. Built by Oregon Volunteers. It served as headquarters for the Volunteers in the region. Location: Walla Walla County. Sited about twenty-five miles of Fort Walla Walla (HBC) on a tributary of Mill Creek.

Mason, Fort (X) (1857) An early defense of the Port Townsend area. A small unfinished hut located at Point Wilson. Location: Jefferson County. Sited at Fort Worden which was built over the post. Also called Fort Wilson.

Maxon Masscre See Mashel Masscare

Medicine Creek Treaty Grounds (M) The first of Isaac Stevens' Washington Territory treaties took place in late December 1854 in a clearing near the mouth of Medicine (now McAllister) Creek on the Nisqually River delta. Location: Thurston County. There are two monuments in the vicinity near where Interstate 5 crosses Medicine Creek near its junction with the Nisqually River; one marker is located near the intersection of 7th SE and Old Pacific Highway; the other is located on private property.

McAllister (X) (1855-1856) Blockhouse. Named after James McAllister who was one of the first whites to be killed in the Yakama Wars. Erected by Washington Volunteers. Location: Pierce County. Sited around the South Prairie area.

McClellan, Captain George USA. (1826-1885) Mexican war. Survey party to select northern rail route (1853). Served with Union forces in the Civil War.

McLoughlin Canyon, Battle of (M) On July 28, 1858 the only battle, in northern Washington Territory, between Indians and whites occurred. Here 160 miners, under the command of David McLoughlin, were ambushed by Okanogan Indians. Fighting lasted several hours and three miners were killed. The next day the miners were able to cross the Okanogan River on rafts. Location: Okanogan County. Marker is located on Highway 97, four miles south of Tonasket and just north of the Janis Bridge on Janis Road.

Miller, Fort (X) (1856) Blockhouse. Named after William Miller of the Washington Volunteers. It was ordered built by Governor Isaac Stevens and served as a supply depot. Location: Thurston County. Sited about twelve miles southeast of Olympia on Tenalquot Prairie.

Mission of the Sacred Heart (SJ, B, SP) For those tribes who could not attend the council at the Ned-whauld River Colonel George Wright arranged for another council here and terms of surrender would be dictated to the tribes. This was also used as the headquarters for the Mullan Road crew. It is also the oldest standing building in Idaho. Location: Kootenai County, Idaho. Twenty miles east of Coeur d' Alene on I-90 at the Old Mission State Park. Also called Cataldo Mission.

Monticello (M) The site of the 1852 meeting that resulted in the petition for the creation of the Territory of Columbia. Location: Cowlitz County. Interpretive signs are at the intersection of 18th Avenue and Olympic Way in Longview.

Muckleshoot Prairie, Battle of See Lemmon's Prairie, Battle of

Muckleshoot Prairie, Camp (M) (1856-1857) Blockhouse. A blockhouse built by US Army troops for the protections of both Indians and whites living in the area. Location: Pierce County. Sited near the confluence of the White and Green River, northeast of Lake Tapps near Highway 164. Also called Fort Slaughter after Lieutenant William Slaughter.

Mullan, Lieutenant John USA (1830-1909) Third Seminole Indian war. Survey party to select a northern rail route (1853); Commander, Indian scouts, Wright campaign (Fall 1858); Supervised construction of military road from Fort Walla Walla to Fort Benton, Montana (1858-1862). Served with Union forces in the Civil War.

Mullan Road (M) Intended as a military road from Fort Walla Walla to Fort Benton, Montana. Named after Lieutenant John Mullan, who supervised the construction from 1858-1862. It became a popular route for people going to the gold fields of

Montana and Idaho in the 1860s. Location: Spokane County. Monuments are located around Spokane. Palouse Highway, just south of 57th Avenue; corner of Sprague and Vista; east 29th, one block west of Glenrose Road; one mile north of Wells Road, on Cheney-Spangle Road; Excelsior Road and Highway 195; 8th Avenue and South Coleman Road.

Na-Chess, Fort See Nechess River, Camp

Naches Pass (X) The pass was one of the principal route through the Cascades. It is closed during the winter. The actual narrow trail, through the Cascades, is now maintained by the US Forest Service. Location: Between Pierce and Yakima Counties.

Nechess River, Camp (USA, M) (1856) The site of Wright's supply depot during the spring and summer of 1856 for operations in and around the Yakama Valley. Location: Yakima County. The fort is located about 10 miles from Yakima on Highway 12 next to the Naches River Water Treatment Plant. Also called Fort Na-Chess and Basket Fort.

Ned-whauld River, Camp on the (X) The site of George Wright's 1858 council with the defeated tribes of the area where Wright dictated surrender terms. Location: Spokane County. Sited south of the Hanging Tree Site on the east side of Kentucky Trails Road between Bradshaw Road and Hays Road. Also called Camp at Latah Creek or Camp at Hangman Creek

Nez Percés, Fort (NWC, HBC, M) (1818-1860)The site of the HBC post at the mouth of the Walla Walla River, and a major stop on the Oregon Trail, was originally built by the NWC before being taken over by the HBC. It is now covered by the backwater behind McNary Dam. Location: Walla Walla Country. A marker is located beside Highway 12, one mile north of the crossing of the Walla Walla, fifteen miles south of Pasco. Also called Fort Walla Walla.

Nisqually, Fort (HBC,B, I, M) (1833-1862) Fort Nisqually was established in 1833 to administer the farms of the Puget Sound Agriculture Company, a subsidiary of the HBC. It was also the principal post for commerce in the Puget Sound region. Location: Pierce County. It was originally built on the Nisqually River delta, but was moved in 1843 to a site a few miles to the north near the present location of the DuPont Company plant. Only a plaque marks the site there, which is about 15 miles south of Tacoma off of I-5. Two remaining original buildings of the fort were moved to Point Defiance Park in Tacoma and the rest of the post was reconstructed. The park is located in Tacoma at the north end of Pearl Street.

Okanogan, Fort (HBC, SP) (1811-186) Originally owned by the Pacific Fur Company this was the first permanent American settlement in the territory. The post was abandoned after the War of 1812 and sold to the North West Company. The HBC later took control and continued its operations until they abandoned it. Location: Okanogan County. Fort Okanogan State Park is about four miles from Brewster.

Ord, Captain Edward USA (1818-1883) Third Artillery. Second Seminole Indian and Mexican War. Rains expedition (November 1855); Wright expedition (Fall 1858), Commander, Fort Vancouver (1861). Served with Union forces during the Civil War.

Olympia (X) (1856) Blockhouse. Built by Washington Volunteers. Location: Thurston County. Sited on Capital Lake Park in Olympia.

Olney, Nathan (1824-1866). Commander, militia attached to Major Haller's expedition against the Indians of the Ward Massacre (Summer 1854); Indian Agent, Oregon Territory (1854-1859); Captain of milita (1855-1856); Talked with Peo-Peo-Mox-Mox before the Battle of Frenchtown; accused of killing Peo-Peo-Mox-Mox (December 1855)

Owhi (?-1858). Yakama Tribe. Battle of Toppenish Creek (October 1855); Participated in the Battle of Seattle (January 1856); Arrived at camp on the Ned-whauld River and was shot trying to escape (October 1858).

Palmer, Joel (1810-1881) Commissary-general, Oregon volunteers and peace commissioner for tribes considering joining the Cayuse (1848-1849); Superintendent of Indian Affairs, Oregon Territory (1853-1857).

Pandosy, Father Charles OMI (1824-1891) Along with Father Louis Joseph D'Herbornez, founded St. Joseph's Mission at Ahtanum Creek (1852); Served as advisor to Kamiakin during the Walla Walla Council (1855); Wrote a dictionary and grammar book of the Yakama Tribe. The working copy was destroyed when soldiers destroyed St. Joseph's Mission during the Rains expedition (November 1855); served as a chaplain for US Army during the Wright expedition (Spring 1856); Stayed at the Colville Mission (1857-1858).

Patterson, Fort See Fort Henderson.

Pender, Lieutenant William USA (1834-1863) First Dragoons. Wright expedition (Fall 1858). Served with Confederate forces in the Civil War.

Peo-Peo-Mox-Mox (?-1855) Walla Walla Tribe. He and several others were taken hostage by militia forces; he was shot and killed while allegedly trying to escape and other hostages were beaten (December 1855).

Pickett, Camp (USA, NPS) See American Camp

Pickett, Captain George USA (1825-1875) Ninth Infantry Regiment. Commander, Fort Bellingham (1856-1859); San Juan Island Dispute (1859); Commander, US forces on San Juan Islands (1859-1861). Served with Confederate forces in the Civil War.

Pike, Fort (X) (1855-1856) Blockhouse. Erected by the central battalion of the Washington Volunteers. Location: Pierce County. Sited somewhere along the White River.

Pine Creek, Battle of See Battle of Tohotomine.

Plante's Ferry (M) The homestead of Antone Plante, a French-Canadian fur trapper, was the site of Governor Isaac Stevens' stormy council with the Spokanes and Couer D' Alenes between December 3-5, 1855. Here Stevens also helped organize two volunteer companies. Location: Spokane County. East of the city of Spokane at12308 E Upriver Drive.

Point Elliot Treaty (M) Site of the second Stevens treaty. is Location: Snohomish County. Location: Snohomish County. Marker at the intersection of 3rd and Lincoln in Mukilteo.

Point No Point Treaty Grounds (M) The site of the treaty with the western Puget Sound tribes. Location: Kitsap County. A small monument located in Hanesville on the grounds of the Point No Point lighthouse.

Port Gamble Cemetery (M) The cemetery contains the grave of the first Navy casualty in the Northwest. The young marine was killed when the frigate *USS Massachusetts* battled with warriors of the British Columbia Haida tribe in 1857. Location: Kitsap County. The cemetery is located in Port Gamble on State Hwy 104.

Posey, Fort (X) (1855-1856)Blockhouse. Erected by the central battalion of the Washington Volunteers. Location: Pierce County. Sited along the White River.

Preston, Fort (X) (1855-1856) Blockhouse. Erected by Washington Volunteers. Location: Pierce County. Sited around the Nisqually-Mashel confluence near Eatonville.

Qualchan (?-1858) Yakama tribe. Accused of leading the group that killed Indian Agent Bolon (September 1855); Lead attack against Connell's Prairie (March 1856); Arrived at camp on the Ned-whauld River and was hanged (September 1858).

Raglan, Fort (X) (185?) Blockhouse. Built by Volunteers. Location: Pierce County. Sited along the Nisqually River.

Rains, Major Gabriel USA (1803-1881) Fourth Infantry Regiment. Second Seminole Indian and Mexican War. Commander, Fort Dalles (1853-1855); Accepted temporary rank of Brigadier-General of Washington Volunteers (November 1855);

Commander, Rains expedition (November 1855). Served with Confederate forces in the Civil War.

Rains, Fort Named after Major Gabriel Rains, Fourth US Infantry. See Cascades, Fort

Riggs, Fort (X) (1855) Blockhouse. Named after Reuben Riggs who had a land claim on the site of the fort. Built by Volunteers. Location: Clark County. Sited on the Columbia River and south of Washougal.

Sales, Fort (X) (1855-1856) This was a settler's cabin that was occupied by soldiers to protect communications between settlements in the Puyallup Valley and Fort Steilacoom. Location: Pierce County. Sited along Sales Road South near Tacoma.

Saint Anne's Mission (D, X) In late winter 400 Washington Volunteers rode to Saint Anne's where they were met by a large force of Cayuse Indians. The Volunteers were soundly defeated and were forced to retreat. The victorious Cayuse then looted the entire settlement and then burned Saint Anne's to the ground. Location: Umatilla County, Oregon. Sited along the Umatilla Creek.

Saint Francis Xaiver Mission (D,M, B) The first permanently established, in 1838, Catholic mission in the present state of

Washington. Location: Lewis County. Located near Highway 505 in Toledo.

Saint Joseph's Mission (OMI, M, B) Isaac Steven's rail route survey party visitied here in 1853. The mission was burned by volunteer and regular troops during the Rains Expedition of 1855. It has since been rebuilt and is still in use today. This was the area that the Yakama chief Kamiakin lived until 1856. Location: Yakima County. The mission is located 14 miles west of Union Gap on Ahtanum Road.

Saint Paul's Mission (SJ,M, B, SP) Mission was built near HBC Fort Colville so that priest could work among the local Indians and HBC workers and visitors. Location: Stevens County. It is located at St. Paul's Mission State Park and is located 3 miles west of Kettle Falls on Highway 395.

Saint Rose Mission (OMI, M) Washington Volunteers burned this mission during the Rains Expedition of 1855. Location: Walla Walla County. One mile west of the Whitman Mission NPS on Highway 12.

San Juan Island, Camp See American Camp

San Juan, Post of See American Camp

Satus Creek, Battle of (M) April 10, 1856. After the Battle of Tasawicks, Thomas Cornelius and his command moved across eastern Washington in an attempt to find Indians to attack. Seeing none Cornelius sent part of his command south for rest and to reconnoiter at the Dalles; he and the rest continued down the Columbia River to HBC Fort Walla Walla and then up the Yakima River. Near the confluence of Satus Creek and the Yakima River nearly 300 Indians, lead by Kamiakin, attacked the volunteers. This five-hour battle yielded little results for either side. Location: Yakima County. Located at the Post Office Part at 1st and Alder. The actual battle site is some 15 miles to the southwest along the lower reaches of Satus Creek before it reaches the Yakima River near the town of Satus.

Seattle, Battle of (X) January 25, 1856. Warriors from the Nisquallies and Upper Yakama tribes attacked the town of Seattle in order to destroy it and then attack Fort Steilacoom. By late morning the *USS Decatur* arrived, opened fired on the attackers and landed sailors and Marines to help defend the town. At night the warriors burned several buildings and retired. Location: King County.

Seattle Blockhouse See Decatur, Fort.

Sheridan, Lieutenant Philip USA (1831-1888) Fourth Infantry Regiment. Rains expedition (November 1855); Battle of

Cascade of Columbia (March 1856). Served with Union forces in the Civil War.

Slaughter, Fort See Muckleshoot Prairie, Camp.

Simcoe, Fort (USA, B, I, SP) (1856-1859) Built in Yakama Country as a base of operations against the Indians and to discourage white settlement in the region. The Yakama Indian Agency later used the post's buildings for its operations. The site of Haller's Defeat in October 1855, is visible from the fort, just to the southeast on the ridges above Toppenish Creek. Location: Yakima County. Fort Simcoe is 5 miles west of the town of White Swan at the end of State Highway 220.

Spalding, Henry (1803-1874) He and his wife Eliza (1807-1851) established a Protestant mission near present day Lewiston, Idaho (1836-1847). Henry Spalding blamed Catholics for the attack on the Whitman Mission. Spalding is also spelled Spaulding.

Spokane, Camp See Spokane, Fort.

Spokane, Fort (NPS, B) (1880-1899) The last USA frontier outpost built in the Northwest and replaced Fort Colville. Post was established, near the junction of the Spokane and Columbia Rivers, when troops from Camp Chelan were transferred here. It later became an Indian School after it was abandoned by the Army.

Location: Lincoln County. Located twenty-one miles north of Davenport on State Highway 25.

Spokane House (M, B, I, SP) (1810-1826) Established by the PFC as a trading post in the region. In 1821 it was acquired by the HBC. Governor Stevens camped and conferred with the Indians in 1853. It is also the final resting place of Jacco Finlay, one of the founders of Spokane House; Finlay is also the only person to be buried in a Washington State Park. Location: Spokane County. Located off of Nine Mile Road, 1/2 mile north of Charles Road.

Spokane Plains, Battle of (M, SP) September 5, 1858. A few days after the Battle of Four Lakes Colonel George Wright took his command north where they were confronted with around 600 warriors. The Indians set fire to the plains but the soldiers dashed through the flames and drove the Indians back into the trees. Wright's artillery then opened fire which wounded Kamiakin. Finally, Dragoons charged the Indian line forcing the warriors to scatter. The soldiers camped that night at the site occupied by Spokane Falls Community College. Location: Spokane County. Near the entrance to Fairchild Air Force Base; about 10 miles west of Spokane on Highway 2.

Steilacoom, Fort (USA, B, I, M) (1849-1868) The lone permanent USA post in the Puget Sound area during the Indian troubles of 1855-1856 was acquired from the HBC to protect the settlers in the area from Indian problems. Location: Pierce County.

Four officers' quarters and part of the old post cemetery remain at the site which are now part of the Western Washington State Hospital. The hospital is located 4 miles west of the city of Steilacoom on Steilacoom Boulevard.

Steptoe, Lieutenant Colonel Edward USA (1816-1865) Ninth Infantry Regiment. Second Seminole and Mexican War. Wright expedition (Spring 1856); Commander, Fort Walla Walla (1856-1858); Battle of Tohotomine (May 1858).

Steptoe's Battlefield See Tohotomine, Battle of.

Stevens, Fort (X) (1855-1856) Blockhouse. Named after Washington Territorial Governor Isaac Stevens. Built by Washington Volunteers of the central battalion and used as a supply depot. Location: Pierce County. Sited on the Yelm Prairie.

Stevens, Isaac (1818-1862). Governor, Washington Territory (1853-1857); Superintendent of Indian Affairs, Washington Territory (1853-1857); Leader of survey party to select northern rail route (1853); Washington Territory delegate to Congress (1857-1858). Served with Union forces in the Civil War.

Tasawicks, Battle of (X) March 13, 1856. 300 soldiers of the First Oregon Volunteers, under their new commander Thomas Cornelius, went after the Walla Walla and Palouse Indians. When the troops reach the Palouse village of Tasawicks, about twenty-five miles upstream on the Snake River where it joins the Columbia River, most of the Indians fled as the command crossed the river in boats. The Volunteers shot four old men and captured two women and a small boy. Location: Franklin County.

Taylor, Fort (X) (1858) Named for Lieutenant Oliver Taylor. The site of the rock bastion supply camp for George Wright's 1858 campaign against the tribes around the Spokane region was located on the left bank of the Snake River at the mouth of the Tucannon River. It is now underwater. Location: Columbia County. Sited next to the mouth of the Tuccanon River, two miles west of the town of Starbuck on Highway 261.

Thomas, Fort (X) (1855) Blockhouse. Named after John Thomas who had a land claim where the blockhouse was built. A temporary blockhouse built by US Army troops. Location: King County. Sited on the south bank of the Green River near the town of Thomas.

Tilton, Fort (X) (1856) Blockhouse. Named after Major James Tilton. A temporary blockhouse built by Washington Volunteers of the northern battalion. Used as a headquarters and supply depot during the Yakama Wars. Location: King County. Sited three miles below the Snoqualmie River Falls.

Timothy (1801-1891) Nez Perce. Rescued Spalding's daughter after the Whitmans were killed (November 1848); Assisted

Lieutenant Colonel Steptoe's expedition across the Snake River (May 1858).

Tohotomine, Battle of (M, SP) May 17,1858. Major Edward Steptoe marched a force of 164 men and Indian scouts towards the mining district of Colville at the request of the miners who were living there. As they reached Tohotomine Creek a force of 1,000 Indians blocked their advance. Steptoe conferred with the tribal leaders and said that his expedition was a peaceful one but realized the conference was in vain. He then ordered his command to retreat southwards. The next day the Indians attacked and were counter-attacked and when evening fell Steptoe found each soldier had just a few rounds of ammunition left. Steptoe wanted to fight the next day but his junior officers convinced him otherwise. They then buried and destroyed everything that wasn't needed for a quiet retreat. Finding an opening in the Indian's position they raced back to the safety Fort Walla Walla. It has never been made clear how Steptoe's command found the opening. Some believe it was pure luck, while other think friendly Indian scouts bribed the hostile forces into creating an opening. Location: Whitman County. The park is in the town of Rosalia, about 38 miles south of Spokane on Highway 195 The ridge top where the soldiers were besieged after the running battle along Tohotomine (now Pine) Creek is marked with a memorial shaft in a small state park. Also called Battle of Pine Creek.

Toppenish Creek, Battle of (X) October 6-8, 1855. In response to the death of Sub-Indian Agent Andrew Bolon Major Gabriel Rains ordered Major Granville Haller, from Fort Dalles, into Yakama country to arrest the murderers. Major Haller marched with 150 men to Toppenish Creek. Here they encountered nearly 1,500 warriors and fought for three days before abandoning all non-essentials equipment and retreating three days, in a running battle, back to Fort Dalles. This was the first battle of the Yakama War. Location: Yakima County. Fort Simcoe State Park is 5 miles west of the town of White Swan at the end of State Hwy 220. The battlefield is visible from the fort, just to the southeast on the ridges above Toppenish Creek.

Townsend, Fort (USA, M, SP) (1856-1861, 1874-1895) Fort Bellingham's companion post on the other side of the sound was established in 1856 to protect settlers in the area from hostile Indians until closed as a military post. It was later re-established as a military post, to protect Indian reservations on the west side of Puget Sound from white encroachment, when Camp Fred Steele was abandoned. Location: Kitsap County. The park is located 5 miles south of Port Townsend off of Highway 115.

Tshimakain Mission Site (M) The first Protestant missionary site in the Spokane region. It was established, in 1838, by Elkanah Walker and Reverend Cushing Eells and their wives. It was abandoned after the attack of the Whitman mission by the Cayuse in 1847. Location: Stevens County. Located on Highway 231, northeast of Ford; near the Chamokane Creek

Twin Buttes, Battle of See Two Buttes, Battle of

Two Buttes, Battle of (M) (November 9, 1855). This skirmish was fought by the soldiers under the command of Major Gabriel Rains in November 1855, along the sides of the gap in the Ahtanum Hills, through which the Yakima River flows. Location: Yakima County. Twin monuments are along the southbound lanes of Highway 97, south of the town of Union Gap. Also called Battle of Twin Buttes.

Tyler, Robert USA (1831-1874). Wright expedition (Fall 1858). Served with Union forces in the Civil War.

Vancouver Barracks See Vancouver, Camp

Vancouver, Camp (USA, I, M, B, NPS) (1849-1947) This site, next to HBC's Fort Vancouver, was the headquarters post for the United States Army's military operations in the Northwest for more than a century. The first USA buildings were leased from HBC. It was originally garrisoned by two companies of the First US Artillery. Very little remains of the pre-1890s except for some extensively remodeled officers' quarters. Location: Clark County. Located at Fort Vancouver National Park in Vancouver. Also called Columbia Barracks, Fort Vancouver and Vancouver Barracks

Vancouver, Fort (HBC, B, NPS) (1824-1860) This was the regional headquarters for the HBC after it moved its operations from HBC's Fort George in Astoria. The Hudson's Bay post operated until its lands were sold to the United States in 1860. Location: Clark County. Located at Fort Vancouver National Park in Vancouver

Vancouver, Fort (USA) See Vancouver, Camp

Waiilatpu, Battle of See Frenchtown, Battle of

Walla Walla Council Grounds (M) The site of the treaty councils of 1855 and 1856 were along the shores of Mill Creek where the city of Walla Walla is located today. Location: Walla Walla County. Monuments commemorating the 1855 event are located on the eastern side of the grounds of Whitman College near downtown Walla Walla near the corner of Stanton and University. A bronze statute of Chief Peo-Peo-Mox-Mox now stands near the corner of Third and Rose Streets in Walla Walla.

Walla Walla, Fort See Nez Perces, Fort

Walla Walla, Fort (USA, B, I, M) (1856-1911) This post was established in 1856 to watch over the various tribes in the region and to discourage white settlements. Units stationed here saw action in every major Northwest Indian war in the late 1800s. A Veterans Administration hospital operates at the site today. The only 1850s-era buildings remaining are the officers' quarters which are now used as doctor's quarters. Location: Walla Walla County. The fort is located south of downtown Walla Walla just off of Highway 125 (Fifteenth Street), near the city limits. The hospital and park have separate entrances.

Ward Massacre Site (M, SP) August 20, 1854. A large number of Shoshones advanced on the twenty-member wagon train of Alexander Ward taking some of their horses. Fighting soon broke out and by evening all the men were dead and the women and children were tortured and raped. Only two boys survived and managed to make their way for help. Major Granville Haller, from Fort Dallas, took sixty-five soldiers and volunteer to search for any more survivors and to punish the Indians. Upon arrival Major Haller ordered the bodies to be buried and the command back to Fort Dalles because the Indians had fled into the mountains and it was too late in the season to go look for them. Location: Canyon County, Idaho. Ward Memorial State Park is west of Boise on old U.S. Highway 20-26 to Middleton Road, at the intersection of Lincoln Road and Middleton Road

Washington, Camp (M) A site where Governor Stevens and Captain George McClellan, along with their military and engineering teams, camped while they were working on northern route railroad survey. Location: Spokane County. Located on Coulee-Hite Road, 9 miles west of Seven Mile Road.

Waters, Fort (X) (1848) Named after Lieutenant Colonel James Water of the Oregon Volunteers. Built by Oregon Volunteers on the grounds of the Whitman Mission ground from the burnt remains of the mission. Location: Walla Walla County. This is located on grounds of the Whitman Mission National Park.

White, Fort (X) (1855-1856) Blockhouse. Named after Captain Joseph White, Second Regiment. Sited at the emigrant crossing of the Puyallup River. Location: Pierce County. Sited near Fort Maloney and the present day shopping center on Meridian Street in Puyallup.

White River, Battle of (X) November 4-7, 1855. Captain Maurice Maloney commanded a force of regular and volunteer troops that was to assist troops marching eastward into Yakama country but found the route over the Cascades blocked with snow. After the command pulled back about 150 Puyallup, Nisqually and Squaxon warriors were sent up the White River to attack Maloney's command. The action was bitter but ended when the Indians retreated, the soldiers pursued them to the Puyallup River where the Indians finally scattered. Location: Pierce County.

Whitman, Marcus (1802-1847). He and his wife Narcissa (1808-1847) founded the first Protestant mission in present day

Washington (1836-1847). They were killed because of a high recovery rate of white patients and a high mortality rate among the Indians. This caused the Indians to believe that the Whitmans were responsible for causing Indian deaths to new diseases in which they had no immunity for.

Whitman Mission (I, M, NP) Site of the first Protestant missionary movement in present day eastern Washington. The destruction of the Mission was the leading cause of the Cayuse War and the ending of the Protestant missions west of the Cascades. Location: Walla Walla County. The site is 6 miles west of Walla Walla just off of Highway 12.

Wilson, Fort See Mason, Fort

Winder, Captain Charles USA (1829-1862). Ninth Infantry Regiment. Battle of Tohotomine (May 1858); Wright expedition (Fall 1858). Served with Confederate forces in the Civil War.

Wright, Colonel George USA (1801-1865) Ninth Infantry Regiment. Second Seminole Indian and Mexican War. Commander, District of Oregon, Department of the Pacific (1855-1861); Commander, Wright expedition (Spring 1856); Commander, Wright expedition (Fall 1858); Appointed commander of the District of Columbia (1865).

Yakima River Battlefield (X) (August 15, 1858). While Colonel George Wright advanced against hostile Indians in eastern

Washington, Major Robert Garnett took his command, from Fort Simcoe. His orders were to support the right flank of Colonel Wright and to attack and punish all hostile Indians. In an early morning attack, by fifteen soldiers, against a Indian camp, yielded in the surrender of seventy Indians by the time the major body arrived. During the attack Lieutenant Jesse Allen was killed by friendly fire. Location: Kittitas County. The site of the only skirmish during Garnett's 1858 campaign is unmarked, but probably occurred somewhere between Cle Elum and Ellensburg.

Yakima Valley (X) (1856) Blockhouse. Built by USA troops. Location: Yakima County. Sited in the Yakima River Valley.

MILITARY TIMELINE OF WASHINGTON TERRITORY[75]

1801

March 4- President Thomas Jefferson speaks of a "rising nation, spread over a wide and fruitful land, traversing all seas...[and] advancing rapidly to destinies beyond the reach of mortal eye"

1804-1805

First overland military expedition to the Northwest (Lewis & Clark). They establish the first US Army post in the region.

1810

Northwest Fur Company establishes Spokane House

1811

The Pacific Fur Company establishes Fort Okanogan. They also build Fort Spokane to compete with the Northwest Fur Company.

1818

US and Britain agree to make the 49th parallel the boundary between the US and Canada for most of the border. Dispute on ownership of the Northwest leaves both countries to resolve their

---

[75] When exact dates are known they are given. When exact dates are unknown then events are listed as specifically as they can; either by month, season or year that they occurred.

differences later on but both agree to joint occupation of the region.

1827

Joint occupancy agreement is renewed indefinitely. A one year notice is required to modify the agreement.

1831

President Andrew Jackson asks the British to reopen negotiations of the area.

1835

November 11- President Andrew Jackson orders US Navy Lieutenant William Slacum to travel to Oregon country to gather information on the conditions of the area.

1836

Marcus Whitman and Henry Spalding, along with their wives, being missionary work at Waiilatpu and Lapwai.

1837

Upon returning to Washington, DC, Lieutenant William Slacum recommends to President Martin Van Buren that the 49th parallel should be the minimum boundary.

1838

Elkanah Walker and Reverend Cushing Eells, along with their wifes, begin missionary work at Tshimakain

Fathers François Blanchet and Modeste Demers arrive at Fort Vancouver

1839

Father François Blanchet establishes Saint Francis Xavier near Toledo.

The Methodists establish a mission at Fort Nisqually.

1842

Outgoing President John Tyler sends a communication to Congress recommending that the US should claim the entire Columbia River drainage system and place the boundary at fifty-four degrees and forty minutes north parallel.

James Polk becomes President and states that "our title to the country of Oregon is clear and unquestionable"

1845

President Polk sends all regular troops stationed in the Northwest south to prepare for war with Mexico; only volunteer forces remain to deal with any British and Indian problems

Lieutenants Warre and Vavasour of the British Army arrive in the Columbia River region with orders to survey the territory in view of possible war with the US

1846
US Congress votes to end joint occupancy in one year of the Northwest

June 12-US and Britain agree to the 49th parallel as the boundary between the US and Canada in the Treaty of Washington

May 13-War begins with Mexico

May 19- Congress authorizes the establishment of military posts along the Oregon Trail and with a new regiment, the Mounted Rifles, to garrison them. Due to the start of the Mexican War the Mounted Rifles are sent to fight the war.

November 3- Military District 10 is formed and administers the area which includes Oregon Territory and as much of the Mexican provinces of California that may be subjected to US law and authority.

1847
5000 people emigrate westwards to the new Oregon Territory. These settlers trample over Cayuse lands, hunt their food and

introduced diseases to the Indians to which the tribes have no immunity to.

February 9- General Stephen Kearny assumes command of Military District 10 and establishes his headquarter at Monterey.

March 4-the *Oregon Spectator* reports the killing of a Mister Newton by Indians in the Umpqua country and several instances of horse stealing by the natives.

May 27- Also, the *Oregon Spectator* blames intoxicants as the cause and called for enforcement of the laws enacted preventing the sale of liquor to the Indians.

July 22-the *Oregon Spectator* publishes a letter from David Ingalls, dated June 18th, from Clatsop Plains, telling of the killing of one Ramsey by Indians and their threats to kill two or three others. According to the letter, the cause of this crime was liquor sold to the Indians by George T. Greer, who is said to be buying quantities of salmon from the natives and plying his customers with liquor.

Joe Lewis and Jacques Finley starts rumors amongst the Cayuse tribe that Doctor Whitman was poisoning their tribe in the guise of medicine.

November 29- several Indians went to the Whitman mission and attack all who were there. Forty-seven men, women and children were taken as captive over the next few days. Father John Brouillet is the first outsider to discover the killings and buries the bodies. A few days later Father Brouillet warns Henry Spalding of the killings and provides him with food and advice to leave the area. Spalding begins to accuse Catholic priests that they deliberately manipulated the Indians to kill the people at the Whitman mission.

1848

Abraham Lincoln is offered the governorship of Oregon Territory.

January 2-after negotiations and trading with the Indians, Peter Skene Ogden manages to obtain the release of all the captives.

The Cayuses attempt to start a regional Indian uprising but many tribes are hesitant to join them and the Nez Perce works against them. A call is sent out for volunteers to help round up the hostiles that were involved in the Whitman Massacre. By February 12 a total of 537 officers and men arrived at The Dalles. Four days later the force under Colonel Cornelius Gilliam begins to move against the Indians.

February 24- Fighting occurs between Indians and militia. Militia forces have five wounded while the Indians have eight killed including Chief Gray Eagle and five wounded including Chief Five Crows.

March 11- Gilliam and his army starts out again. Captain McKay and others who were ill, left for the Willamette Valley which leaves a force that numbered 268 officers and men. They continue toward the Cayuse camp. It was then that they were ambushed by four hundred Palouse, allies of the Cayuse. The troops were heavily outnumber and kept fighting as they moved backwards in an attempt to reach a strategic point at the river. Finally, Captain William Shaw with 20 picked men is ordered to attempt to reach the river and secure a vantage point. By running their horses for 3/4 of a mile they managed to outrace the hostiles to the vantage point.

March 20-Colonel Gilliam camps on the Umatilla River. There, while pulling a halter-rope from a wagon-bed, the rope is caught on a gun trigger, resulting in the death of Gilliam. One of the consequences of Gilliam's death was that an officer named Lieutenant Rogers intercepts a shipment of firearms and ammunition that is intended for Catholic Indians for their needs and protection against their enemies of the Blackfoot Indians. Rogers then accuses the Catholics saying that the weapons are intended for the extermination of the Protestants in the area.

Later in the year the militia decides to abandon the campaign for the season.

August 13- Oregon Territory is created.

August 31- The Army reorganizes its administration and the Oregon Territory becomes Military Department 11 with its headquarters at Fort Vancouver.

1849

May 13-Companies L and M of the First US Artillery arrive at the Hudson's Bay Company's Fort Vancouver and began to establish Camp Vancouver.

October- The Regiment of Mounted Rifles arrives at Camp Vancouver but are later moved eastward to establish Camp Drum on the Columbia River.

1850

Donation Land Claims Act is enacted by US Congress

Early Spring- Having failed to convince the Americans that all murders of the Whitman Massacre were dead the Cayuse Chiefs find five men who agreed to go to Oregon City to try and convince the Americans that all the murders were truly dead. When they arrive they are arrested and charged with the murders.

May 27- A trial is held and the Cayuse Indians are found guilty. Upon hearing the verdict they request to see a Catholic priest.

June 3- The Cayuse prisoners attend Mass and are baptized and confirmed in the Catholic faith. They are then lead to the gallows and hanged.

Many Indian tribes regret not joining in to force the white settlers out of the region.

1851

August 29- Cowlitz Convention petitions Congress to create a new region north of the Columbia River to be called the Territory of Columbia.

1852

September 22-US Fourth Infantry Regiment, under the command of Lieutenant Colonel Benjamin Bonneville, arrive for garrison duty in the Northwest.

November 25-The Monticello Convention meets and affirms the need for the naming of the Territory of Columbia.

1853

February 10-Congress approves a new territory but calls it Washington.

March 2-Washington Territory is created.
Isaac Stevens is appointed first Territorial Governor and Superintendent of Indian Affairs.

Father Charles Pandosy writes a letter to Father Toussaint Mesplie warning that Indian tribes are uniting against the Americans to drive them off their land; report is ignored and Father Pandosy is labeled an alarmist by the Americans.

Companies L and M of the First US Artillery are relieved of garrison duties and ordered to the east coast.

1854

Lieutenant Colonel Bonneville is promoted to the rank of Colonel and given command of an infantry regiment in the Department of New Mexico; Major Gabriel Rains is named Commander, District of Oregon.

August 20- The Alexander Ward party is attacked along the Oregon Trail. Eighteen out of a party of twenty are killed and they remaining two are left for dead. Major Granville Haller, commanding Fort Dalles, is sent to see if there are any survivors and to punish the Indians who attacked the party

December 26- The Council at Medicine Creek concludes with a treaty being signed.

1855

January 22- Treaty of Point Elliot is signed in present day Mukilteo.

January 26- Point No Point Treaty is signed on the northern tip of the Kitsap Peninsula.

May 29-June 11- First Walla Walla Council is held by Governor Stevens

July- Major Granville Haller is sent back to the area where the Ward party was killed with orders to find the Indians who were responsible for the attack. He finds several of them and orders a trial. The Indians are found guilty and hanged over where the Ward party was buried. Haller then orders his command to find the rest of the Indians; over the next few months his command covers over 1,500 miles and kills a total of eighteen Indians.

September- Gold is discovered in Colville area

September 23-Indian Sub-Agent Andrew Bolon is killed by Yakama Indians while he was investigating reports of conflicts between miners and the Yakama tribe.

October 3- Upon his return to Fort Dalles Major Granville Haller is ordered to investigate and bring back the murders of Bolon. His command consists of 84 Regulars and about 20 Indian guides. The expedition heads towards Saint Joseph's Mission at Ahtanum Creek where Chief Kamiakin is said to be.

October 6-8- In Yakama Territory Major Haller's force is initially surrounded by 200 warriors but this number grows over the next few days to about 1,500 Indians. Haller is surrounded and forced to fight. Seeing that his position would be overran he decides to retreat. The command returns back to Fort Dalles on October 10.

October 31- Major Gabrielle Rains mounts an expedition of about 700 Regular infantry, artillery, dragoons and Oregon and Washington Volunteers in which to punish the Yakama tribe.

November 3- Major General John Wool, commanding the Department of the Pacific, requests more troops to be sent to the Pacific.

November 4-7- Battle of White River. A mixed force of regular and volunteer troop make contact with 150 Indians near the White River.

November 9-Battle of Two Buttes. Army and Yakama Indians make contact with each other and the outcome is inconclusive for both sides.

November 13- Army units arrive at Saint Joseph's Mission and find gun powder buried in the garden. Suspecting the priest of aiding the Indians the Army loots and burns down the Mission. A few days later volunteer soldiers burn the Immaculate Conception Mission on Manastash Creek. The Holy Cross Mission in the lower Ahtanum Valley is also burned sometime during the expedition.

November 24- Rains expedition officially ends.

December 1- The War Department proposes to send the Ninth Infantry Regiment to the Department of the Pacific.

December 3-5- Governor Isaac Stevens meets with various tribes at Plante's Ferry.

December 7-10- Battle of Frenchtown. Lieutenant Colonel James Kelly, commanding the First Oregon Volunteers, leaves Fort Dalles on December 2 with about 350 men in the direction of Hudson's Bay Company's Fort Walla Walla. On December 4 at the confluence of the Touchet and Walla Walla Rivers Kelly met with Chief Peo-peo-mox-mox of the Walla Walla Tribe. Kelly suspecting trickery held the chief and several others as hostage. Moving further up the Walla Walla River the volunteers, on December 7, found themselves outnumbers by three to one and a moving battle started. By December 10 the volunteers had repulsed several attacks and were able to threaten the flanks of the Indians who were forced to leave the field. Chief Peo-peo-mox-mox and other hostages were killed as they allegedly tried to flee. The Walla Wallas and Cayuse suffered 100 casualties and the militia suffered 26 casualties.

1856
January 21-US Ninth Infantry, under the command of Colonel George Wright, arrives at Fort Vancouver to reinforce the Fourth Infantry and to make war against the Indians.

March 1- After US forces move from their camp on the Muckleshoot Prairie to another camp on Lemmon's Prairie Indians forces attack. Chief Kanaskat is captured and killed.

March 13- After spending the winter in the Walla Walla Valley the First Oregon Volunteers, now under the command of Thomas Cornelius, move against the Walla Walla and Palouse Indians. The unit crosses the Snake River to attack the Palouse village of Tasawicks. Finding most of the inhabitants had fled during the river crossing the advance guard killed four old men who could not keep up with the rest; the command manages to capture three other people.

March 28- Chief Chenowith, and others, are tried and hung for their part of the Battle of the Cascades.

March 31- In a series of patrols around the Nisqually and Mashel Rivers, Volunteers attack Indian camps of mostly unarmed women and children.

April 10- After the Battle of Tasawick the Oregon Volunteers continued eastward in an attempt to find Walla Walla and Palouse Indians. Near the confluence of Satus Creek and the Yakima River 300 Yakamas, lead by Chief Kamiakin, attacks the Volunteers. After about five hours of fighting the Indians withdraw and the Volunteers go to Fort Dalles.

April 28- Acting under orders to move into Yakama Territory Colonel George Wright commands a force of about 500 men northwards to the Naches River. Finding it impassable for infantry due to the spring run-off he establishes Fort Nechess as a supply base of operations in the area. He orders Lieutenant Colonel Edward Steptoe and Major Robert Garnett commands to join him. When they arrived Colonel Wright has about 750 soldiers with him.

May 11-Colonel George Wright and Lieutenant Colonel Silas Casey announce that the war in the Puget Sound region is over.

June 17- The Naches River is bridged and Wright marches north and west. Lieutenant Colonel Steptoe is left in command of Fort Naches. Wright moves up to the Wenatchee Valley where he a conference with some of the Indian leaders in which they expressed a desire for peace. Wright takes Chief Teias and his family as hostages and returns to Fort Naches on July 21. The campaign is finished.

July 17- In early July 400 Washington Volunteers, under the command of Lieutenant Colonel Benjamin Shaw, march into Oregon Territory. In the Grande Ronde Valley they come upon 300 Walla Walla, Cayuse, DesChutes, Palouse and Umatilla Indians. Shaw sends a Nez Perce scout to talk to them but the scout comes galloping back saying he heard one Cayuse order others to shoot him. Shaw orders his men to attack who kill over 40 Indians and wounded many more. They also destroy the village and captured 200 horses.

August 2- Major General John Wool announces that no whites except Hudson's Bay Company employees and missionaries are to be allowed in the area east of the Cascades.

August 8- Wright assigns Major Robert Garnett to establish Fort Simcoe in Yakama Indian Territory.

August 20-Lieutenant Colonel Edward Steptoe leads a supply train into the Walla Walla Valley to establish a military post.

September 11-17 The Second Walla Walla Council is convened with tribal leaders demanding that the treaties should be cancelled and settlers kept off Indian lands.

September 15- Lieutenant Colonel Edward Steptoe reported that he has selected a position "on Mills creek for the military post. It is five miles below Whitman's old mill site, is directly on the trails from the Nez Percés, Spokane, and Palouse country, and controls the entire valley."

1858

January 12- Lieutenant Colonel Edward Steptoe receives orders from the Department of the Pacific to watch the Indians in the area because it appears that "through the Mormons the Indians are being inclined to hostility, and that a conflict in Utah may be the signal for trouble on the frontier, and it is not improbable that the Mormons may move north."

February 19- Chief Leschi is hanged near Fort Steilacoom.

April 17- Lieutenant Colonel Edward Steptoe reports to the Department that "there appears to be so much excitement amongst the Pelouse and Spokane Indians as to make an expedition to the north advisable...[and] some forty persons living at Colville recently petitioned for the presence of troops at that place as they believed their lives and property to be in danger from hostile Indians."

April 20- Letter from the General Council of the Oblates in France ordering that the Yakama Missions to be closed is received by the priests in Washington Territory.

May 6- Lieutenant Colonel Edward Steptoe leads a force of over 150 men from Fort Walla Walla to Colville.

May 16- Lieutenant Colonel Edward Steptoe finds the path he wants to take is block by a large number of Indians. Steptoe orders his men to a better position. Early the next morning the expedition retreats and barely made three miles when the Indians appearand start their attack that begins a ten-hour running battle. That night Steptoe and his officers decide to retreat before sunrise.

Abandoning all that was not needed the command slips through Indian lines and make it back to Fort Walla Walla by May 20.

July 28- Okanogan-area Indians, speculated to be under the command of Chiefs Moses, Tonasket and Sarsapkin ambush about 160 miners under the direction of David McLouglin. Fighting takes place over several hours and three miners were killed.

August 7- Colonel George Wright leads a 700-man force northwards from Fort Walla Walla to punish the Indians that defeated Lieutenant Colonel Edward Steptoe's force.

August 10- Major Robert Garnett leads a 300-man force from Fort Simcoe. This force moves northwards into central Washington Territory and has orders to protect Colonel Wright's left flank.

August 15- In the only battle of the expedition sixteen men of Major Robert Garnett's force attempt to surround and capture and Indian village. One Indian is killed but sixty-one people are captured along with eighty-five horses and cattle. Several Indians are also shot after it was learned that they were participants in attacks upon some miners.

September 1- Colonel George Wright defeats a large Indian force at the Battle of Four Lakes.

September 5- Colonel George Wright engages the Indians at the Battle of Spokane Plains.

September 8- The Army captures nearly 900 Indian horses. Starting on the 9th they begin to kill over 700 horses at what is called Horse Slaughter Camp. This action, along with the defeats of the previous week, finally breaks the fighting spirit of the Indians.

September 13-The Army reorganizes itself and the Department of Oregon was created. The Department is responsible for Oregon and Washington Territory. General William Harney is the first commander but arrives after the Wright-Garnett campaign is completed.

September 15- Major Robert Garnett's command returns to Fort Simcoe.

September 23-26- Colonel George Wright encamps at the Ned-Whauld River where he accepts the surrender of the Spokane Tribe.

September 24- Chief Qualchan arrives at the Camp on the Ned-whauld River and was promptly hanged.

September 30- Colonel George Wright writes "The war is closed. Peace is restored with the Spokanes, Coeur d' Alenes and

Pelouses. After a vigorous campaign the Indians have been entirely subdued, and were most happy to accept such terms of peace as I might dictate."

October 2- Chief Owhi is killed while attempting to escape.

October 5- The Wright-Garnett campaign finishes as Colonel George Wright's command returns to Fort Walla Walla.

1859
March 18-Lieutenant John Mullan is ordered to begin construction of a wagon road, beginning near Fort Walla Walla to Fort Benton, Missouri.

July 29- Secretary of Washington Territory Charles Mason dies in Olympia, Washington Territory.

1860
General William Harney is relieved of command of the Department of Oregon and turns command over to Colonel George Wright.

October 17- General Newman Clarke dies in San Francisco, California.

1861-1865

US Army troops investigate disturbances and disputes between white settlers and Indians in eastern Washington and Idaho Territories. In 1863 Fort Boise is established to protect travelers along the Oregon Trail.

1861

July 13- General Robert Garnett dies at Corrick's Ford in West Virginia.

1862

August 9- General Charles Winder dies during the Battle of Cedar Mountain, Virginia.

September 1- General Isaac Stevens is killed at the Battle of Chantilly, Virginia.

1863

March 4-The Territory of Idaho is created from Washington Territory

July 18- General William Pender dies Stauton, Virginia.

1864

August 24- James Archer dies in Richmond, Virginia.

1865

April 17- Edward Steptoe dies in Lynchburg, Virginia.

July 27- The Military Division of the Pacific is created along with the Department of the Columbia. The Department of the Columbia replaces the District of Oregon and is responsible for Oregon, the Territories of Washington and Idaho and the expanded Department of California.

July 30- General George Wright drowns on his way to assume command of the new Department of the Columbia. Colonel George Currey assumes temporary command of the Department.

November 20- Lieutenant Colonel John Drake takes command of the Department of the Columbia.

December 21- Major General Frederick Steele takes command of the Department of the Columbia.

1866

September 28- Nathan Olney dies at Fort Simcoe, Washington Territory.

December 11-Brigadier General George Crook takes command of the Department of the Columbia.

1867

The Territorial Legislature petitions Congress to admit Washington to statehood.

1868

July 15- Guert Gansevoort dies in Schenectady, New York.

1869

Major General Edward Canby takes command of the Department of the Columbia.

November 10- James Wool dies in Troy, New York.

1870

July 1- The Department of Alaska is discontinued and absorbed by the Department of the Columbia.

1873

Upon the death of General Canby during the Modoc wars Colonel Alvan Gillem assumes command of the Department of the Columbia. Later in the year Colonel Jefferson Davis takes command of the Department.

1874

Brigadier General Oliver Howard takes command of the Department of the Columbia.

August 3- Henry Spalding dies in Lapwai, Idaho.

December 1- Robert Tyler dies in Boston, Massachusetts.

1875

June- The part of the Territory of Idaho that lays east of the extension of the western boundary of Utah is detached from the Department of the Columbia and added to the Department of the Platte.

July 30- George Pickett dies at Norfolk, Virginia.

1876

January 6- Chief Lawyer dies

June 10- Thomas English dies in Philadelphia, Pennsylvania.

1877

April- Chief Kamiakin dies around the Rock Lake, Washington area.

November 21- Rev. Elkanah Walker dies in Forest Grove, Oregon.

1880

General Nelson Miles becomes commander of the Department of the Columbia.

1881

June 9- Joel Palmer dies in Dayton, Oregon.

September 6- Gabriel Rains dies in Aiken, South Carolina.

1882

January 22- Silas Casey dies in Brooklyn, New York.

1883

June 18- Archbishop François Blanchet dies in St. Paul, Oregon.

July 22- Edward Ord dies in Havana, Cuba.

1884

February 5- Father John Brouillet dies at the Devil's Lake Indian Agency, Dakota Territory.

October 16- Benjamin Alvord dies in Washington, DC.

1885

General John Gibbon becomes the last commander of the Department of the Columbia.

July 23- Ulysses Grant dies at Mount McGregor, New York.

1886

September 6- Colonel Lewis Hunt dies at Fort Union, New Mexico.

1887

August 5-Calvin Hale dies in Olympia, Washington

1888

August 5- Philip Sheridan dies in Nonquitt, Massachusetts

1889

May 9- William Harney dies in Orlando, Florida.

November 11- Washington becomes a state.

1891

Chief Timothy dies sometime during the year.

February 6- Father Charles Pandosy dies near Kelowna, British Columbia.

July 3- The Military Division of the Pacific is discontinued. The Department of the Columbia now reports directly to the War Department.

1892

January 14- Chief Garry dies near Spokane, Washington.

May 28, Father Casimir Chirouse dies in Mission City, British Columbia.

1893

February 16- Rev. Cushing Eells dies in Seattle, Washington.

1895

October 14- Erasmus Keyes dies in Nice, France.

1897

May 2- Granville Haller dies in Seattle, Washington.

1898

January 16- Christopher Augur dies Washington, DC.

1899

March 4- Henry Davidson dies in Livermore, California.

1900

June 19- Fr. Joseph Joset dies at the Mission of the Sacred Heart in Idaho

VARIOUS TREATIES OF WASHINGTON TERRITORY

Treaty of Medicine Creek, 1854

Articles of agreement and convention made and concluded on the She-nah-nam, or Medicine Creek, in the Territory of Washington, this twenty-sixth day of December, in the year one thousand eight hundred and fifty-four, by Isaac I. Stevens, governor and superintendent of Indian affairs of the said Territory, on the part of the United States, and the undersigned chiefs, head-men, and delegates of the Nisqually, Puyallup, Steilacoom, Squawskin, S'Homamish, Stehchass, T'Peeksin, Squi-aitl, and Sa-heh-wamish tribes and bands of Indians, occupying the lands lying round the head of Puget's Sound and the adjacent inlets, who, for the purpose of this treaty, are to be regarded as one nation, on behalf of said tribes and bands, and duly authorized by them.

ARTICLE 1
The said tribes and bands of Indians hereby cede, relinquish, and convey to the United States, all their right, title, and interest in and to the lands and country occupied by them, bounded and described as follows, to wit: Commencing at the point on the eastern side of Admiralty Inlet, known as Point Pully, about midway between Commencement and Elliott Bays; thence running in a southeasterly direction, following the divide between the waters of the Puyallup and Dwamish, or White Rivers, to the summit of the Cascade Mountains; thence southerly, along the summit of said range, to a point opposite the main source of the Skookum Chuck Creek; thence to and down said creek, to the coal mine; thence northwesterly, to the summit of the Black Hills; thence northerly, to the upper forks of the Satsop River; thence northeasterly, through the portage known as Wilkes's Portage, to Point Southworth, on the western side of Admiralty Inlet; thence around the foot of Vashon's Island, easterly and southeasterly, to the place of beginning.

ARTICLE 2
There is, however, reserved for the present use and occupation of the said tribes and bands, the following tracts of land, viz: The small island called Klah-che-min, situated opposite the mouths of Hammerslev's and Totten's Inlets, and separated from Hartstene Island by Peale's Passage, containing about two sections of land by estimation; a square tract containing two sections, or twelve hundred and eighty acres, on Puget's Sound, near the mouth of the She-nah-nam Creek, one mile west of the meridian line of the United States land survey, and a square tract containing two sections, or twelve hundred and eighty acres, lying on the south side of Commencement Bay; all which tracts shall be set apart, and, so far as necessary, surveyed and marked out for their exclusive use; nor shall any white man be permitted to reside upon the same without permission of the tribe and the superintendent or agent. And the said tribes and bands agree to remove to and settle upon the same within one year after the ratification of this treaty, or sooner if the means are furnished them. In the mean time, it shall be lawful for them to reside upon any ground not in the actual claim and occupation of citizens of the United States, and upon any ground claimed or occupied, if with the permission of the owner or claimant. If necessary for the public convenience, roads may be run through their reserves, and, on the other hand, the right of way with free access from the same to the nearest public highway is secured to them.

ARTICLE 3
The right of taking fish, at all usual and accustomed grounds and stations, is further secured to said Indians in common with all citizens of the Territory, and of erecting temporary houses for the purpose of curing, together with the privilege of hunting, gathering roots and berries, and pasturing their horses on open and unclaimed lands: Provided, however, That they shall not take shellfish from any beds staked or cultivated by citizens, and that they shall alter all stallions not intended for breeding-horses, and shall keep up and confine the latter.

ARTICLE 4
In consideration of the above session, the United States agree to pay to the said tribes and bands the sum of thirty-two thousand five

hundred dollars, in the following manner, that is to say: For the first year after the ratification hereof, three thousand two hundred and fifty dollars; for the next two years, three thousand dollars each year; for the next three years, two thousand dollars each year; for the next four years fifteen hundred dollars each year; for the next five years twelve hundred dollars each year; and for the next five years one thousand dollars each year; all which said sums of money shall be applied to the use and benefit of the said Indians, under the direction of the President of the United States, who may from time to time determine, at his discretion, upon what beneficial objects to expend the same. And the superintendent of Indian affairs, or other proper officer, shall each year inform the President of the wishes of said Indians in respect thereto.

ARTICLE 5
To enable the said Indians to remove to and settle upon their aforesaid reservations, and to clear, fence, and break up a sufficient quantity of land for cultivation, the United States further agree to pay the sum of three thousand two hundred and fifty dollars, to be laid out and expended under the direction of the President, and in such manner as he shall approve.

ARTICLE 6
The President may hereafter, when in his opinion the interests of the Territory may require, and the welfare of the said Indians be promoted, remove them from either or all of said reservations to such other suitable place or places within said Territory as he may deem fit, on remunerating them for their improvements and the expenses of their removal, or may consolidate them with other friendly tribes or bands. And he may further, at his discretion, cause the whole or any portion of the lands hereby reserved, or of such other land as may be selected in lieu thereof, to be surveyed into lots, and assign the same to such individuals or families as are willing to avail themselves of the privilege, and will locate on the same as a permanent home, on the same terms and subject to the same regulations as are provided in the sixth article of the treaty with the Omahas, so far as the same may be applicable. Any substantial improvements heretofore made by any Indian, and which he shall be compelled to abandon in consequence of this

treaty, shall be valued under the direction of the President, and payment to be made accordingly thereof.

ARTICLE 7
The annuities of the aforesaid tribes and bands shall not be taken to pay the debts of individuals.

ARTICLE 8
The aforesaid tribes and bands acknowledge their dependence on the Government of the United States, and promise to be friendly with all citizens thereof, and pledge themselves to commit no depredations on the property of such citizens. And should any one or more of them violate this pledge, and the fact be satisfactorily proved before the agent, the property taken shall be returned, or in default thereof, or if injured or destroyed, compensation may be made by the Government out of their annuities. Nor will they make war on any other tribe except in self-defence, but will submit all matters of difference between them and other Indians to the Government of the United States, or its agent, for decision, and abide thereby. And if any of the said Indians commit any depredations on any other Indians within the Territory, the same rule shall prevail as that prescribed in this article, in cases of depredations against citizens. And the said tribes agree not to shelter or conceal offenders against the laws of the United States, but to deliver them up to the authorities for trail.

ARTICLE 9
The above tribes and bands are desirous to exclude from their reservations the use of ardent spirits, and to prevent their people from drinking the same; and therefore it is provided, that any Indian belonging to said tribes, who is guilty of bringing liquor into said reservations, or who drinks liquor, may have his or her proportion of the annuities withheld from him or her for such time as the President may determine.

ARTICLE 10
The United States further agree to establish at the general agency for the district of Puget's Sound, within one year from the ratification hereof, and to support, for a period of twenty years, an agricultural and industrial school, to be free to children of the said

tribes and bands, in common with those of the other tribes of said district, and to provide the said school with a suitable instructor or instructors, and also to provide a smithy and carpenter's shop, and furnish them with the necessary tools, and employ a blacksmith, carpenter, and farmer, for the term of twenty years, to instruct the Indians in their respective occupations. And the United States further agree to employ a physician to reside at the said central agency, who shall furnish medicine and advice to their sick, and shall vaccinate them; the expenses of the said school, shops, employees, and medical attendance, to be defrayed by the United States, and not deducted from the annuities.

ARTICLE 11
The said tribes and bands agree to free all slaves now held by them, and not to purchase or acquire others hereafter.

ARTICLE 12
The said tribes and bands finally agree not to trade at Vancouver's Island, or elsewhere out of the dominions of the United States; nor shall foreign Indians be permitted to reside in their reservations without consent of the superintendent or agent.

ARTICLE 13
This treaty shall be obligatory on the contracting parties as soon as the same shall be ratified by the President and Senate of the United States.
In testimony whereof, the said Isaac I. Stevens, governor and superintendent of Indian Affairs, and the undersigned chiefs, headmen, and delegates of the aforesaid tribes and bands, have hereunto set their hands and seals at the place and on the day and year hereinbefore written.

Isaac I. Stevens, (L.S.)
Governor and Superintendent Territory of Washington.
Qui-ee-metl, his x mark. (L.S.)
Sno-ho-dumset, his x mark. (L.S.)
Lesh-high, his x mark. (L.S.)
Slip-o-elm, his x mark. (L.S.)
Kwi-ats, his x mark. (L.S.)
Stee-high, his x mark. (L.S.)

Di-a-keh, his x mark. (L.S.)
Hi-ten, his x mark. (L.S.)
Squa-ta-hun, his x mark. (L.S.)
Kahk-tse-min, his x mark. (L.S.)
Sonan-o-yutl, his x mark. (L.S.)
Kl-tehp, his x mark. (L.S.)
Sahl-ko-min, his x mark. (L.S.)
T'bet-ste-heh-bit, his x mark. (L.S.)
Tcha-hoos-tan, his x mark. (L.S.)
Ke-cha-hat, his x mark. (L.S.)
Spee-peh, his x mark. (L.S.)
Swe-yah-tum, his x mark. (L.S.)
Cha-achsh, his x mark. (L.S.)
Pich-kehd, his x mark. (L.S.)
S'Klah-o-sum, his x mark. (L.S.)
Sah-le-tatl, his x mark. (L.S.)
See-lup, his x mark. (L.S.)
E-la-kah-ka, his x mark. (L.S.)
Slug-yeh, his x mark. (L.S.)
Hi-nuk, his x mark. (L.S.)
Ma-mo-nish, his x mark. (L.S.)
Cheels, his x mark. (L.S.)
Knutcanu, his x mark. (L.S.)
Bats-ta-kobe, his x mark. (L.S.)
Win-ne-ya, his x mark. (L.S.)
Klo-out, his x mark. (L.S.)
Se-uch-ka-nam, his x mark. (L.S.)
Ske-mah-han, his x mark. (L.S.)
Wuts-un-a-pum, his x mark. (L.S.)
Quuts-a-tadm, his x mark. (L.S.)
Quut-a-heh-mtsn, his x mark. (L.S.)
Yah-leh-chn, his x mark. (L.S.)
To-lahl-kut, his x mark. (L.S.)
Yul-lout, his x mark. (L.S.)
See-ahts-oot-soot, his x mark. (L.S.)
Ye-takho, his x mark. (L.S.)
We-po-it-ee, his x mark. (L.S.)
Kah-sld, his x mark. (L.S.)
La'h-hom-kan, his x mark. (L.S.)
Pah-how-at-ish, his x mark. (L.S.)

Swe-yehm, his x mark. (L.S.)
Sah-hwill, his x mark. (L.S.)
Se-kwaht, his x mark. (L.S.)
Kah-hum-klt, his x mark. (L.S.)
Yah-kwo-bah, his x mark. (L.S.)
Wut-sah-le-wun, his x mark. (L.S.)
Sah-ba-hat, his x mark. (L.S.)
Tel-e-kish, his x mark. (L.S.)
Swe-keh-nam, his x mark. (L.S.)
Sit-oo-ah, his x mark. (L.S.)
Ko-quel-a-cut, his x mark. (L.S.)
Jack, his x mark. (L.S.)
Keh-kise-bel-lo, his x mark. (L.S.)

Treaty of Point Elliott, 1855

Articles of agreement and convention made and concluded at Muckl-te-oh, or Point Elliott, in the territory of Washington, this twenty-second day of January, eighteen hundred and fifty-five, by Isaac I. Stevens, governor and superintendent of Indian affairs for the saidTerritory, on the part of the United States, and the undersigned chiefs, head-men and delegates of the Dwamish, Suquamish, Sk-kahl-mish, Sam-ahmish, Smalh-kamish, Skope-ahmish, St-kah-mish, Snoqualmoo, Skai-wha-mish, N'Quentl-ma-mish, Sk-tah-le-jum, Stoluck-wha-mish, Sno-ho-mish, Skagit, Kik-i-allus, Swin-a-mish, Squin-ah-mish, Sah-ku-mehu, Noo-wha-ha, Nook-wa-chah-mish, Mee-see-qua-guilch, Cho-bah-ah-bish, and othe allied and subordinate tribes and bands of Indians occupying certain lands situated in said Territory of Washington, on behalf of said tribes, and duly authorized by them.

ARTICLE 1
The said tribes and bands of Indians hereby cede, relinquish, and convey to the United States all their right, title, and interest in and to the lands and country occupied by them, bounded and described as follows: Commencing at a point on the eastern side of Admiralty Inlet, known as Point Pully, about midway between Commencement and Elliott Bays; thence eastwardly, running along the north line of lands heretofore ceded to the United States by the Nisqually, Puyallup, and other Indians, to the summit of the

Cascade range of mountains; thence northwardly, following the summit of said range to the 49th parallel of north latitude; thence west, along said parallel to the middle of the Gulf of Georgia; thence through the middle of said gulf and the main channel through the Canal de Arro to the Straits of Fuca, and crossing the same through the middle of Admiralty Inlet to Suquamish Head; thence southwesterly, through the peninsula, and following the divide between Hood's Canal and Admiralty Inlet to the portage known as Wilkes' Portage; thence northeastwardly, and following the line of lands heretofore ceded as aforesaid to Point Southworth, on the western side of Admiralty Inlet, and thence around the foot of Vashon's Island eastwardly and southeastwardly to the place of beginning, including all the islands comprised within said boundaries, and all the right, title, and interest of the said tribes and bands to any lands within the territory of the United States.

ARTICLE 2

There is, however, reserved for the present use and occupation of the said tribes and bands the following tracts of land, viz:the amount of two sections, or twelve hundred and eighty acres, surrounding the small bight at the head of Port Madison, called by the Indians Noo-sohk-um; the amount of two sections, or twelve hundred and eighty acres, on the north side Hwhomish Bay and the creek emptying into the same called Kwilt-seh-da, the peninsula at the southeastern end of Perry's Island, called Shais-quihl, and the island called Chah-choo-sen, situated in the Lummi River at the point of separation of the mouths emptying respectively into Bellingham Bay and the Gulf of Georgia. All which tracts shall be set apart, and so far as necessary surveyed and marked out for their exclusive use; nor shall any white man be permitted to reside upon the same without permission of the said tribes or bands, and of the superintendent or agent, but, if necessary for the public convenience, roads may be run through the said reserves, the Indians being compensated for any damage thereby done them.

ARTICLE 3

There is also reserved from out the lands hereby ceded the amount of thirty-six sections, or one township of land, on the northeastern shore of Port Gardner, and north of the mouth of Snohomish River, including Tulalip Bay and the before-mentioned Kwilt-seh-da

Creek, for the purpose of establishing thereon an agricultural and industrial school, as hereinafter mentioned and agreed, and with a view of ultimately drawing thereto and settling thereon all the Indians living west of the Cascade Mountains in said Territory. Provided, however, That the President may establish the central agency and general reservation at such other point as he may deem for the benefit of the Indians.

ARTICLE 4
The said tribes and bands agree to remove to and settle upon the said first above-mentioned reservations within one year after the ratification of this treaty, or sooner, if the means are furnished them. In the mean time it shall be lawful for them to reside upon any land not in the actual claim and occupation of citizens of the United States, and upon any land claimed or occupied, if with the pe-mission of the owner.

ARTICLE 5
The right of taking fish at usual and accustomed grounds and stations is further secured to said Indians in common with all citizens of the Territory, and of erecting temporary houses for the purpose of curing, together with the privilege of hunting and gathering roots and berries on open and unclaimed lands. Provided, however, That they shall not take shell-fish from any beds staked or cultivated by citizens.

ARTICLE 6
In consideration of the above cession, the United States agree to pay to the said tribes and bands the sum of one hundred and fifty thousand dollars, in the following manner - - that is to say: For the first year after the ratification hereof, fifteen thousand dollars; for the next two year, twelve thousand dollars each year; for the next three years, ten thousand dollars each year; for the next four years, seven thousand five hundred dollars each years; for the next five years, six thousand dollars each year; and for the last five years, four thousand two hundred and fifty dollars each year. All which said sums of money shall be applied to the use and benefit of the said Indians, under the direction of the President of the United States, who may, from time to time, determine at his discretion upon what beneficial objects to expend the same; and the

superintendent of Indian affairs, or other proper officer, shall each year inform the President of the wishes of said Indians in respect thereto.

ARTICLE 7
The President may hereafter, when in his opinion the interests of the Territory shall require and the welfare of the said Indians be promoted, remove them from either or all of the special reservations hereinbefore make to the said general reservation, or such other suitable place within said Territory as he may deem fit, on remunerating them for their improvements and the expenses of such removal, or may consolidate them with other friendly tribes or bands; and he may further at his discretion cause the whole or any portion of the lands hereby reserved, or of such other land as may be selected in lieu thereof, to be surveyed into lots, and assign the same to suc individuals or families as are willing to avail themselves of the privilege, and will locate on the same as a permanent home on the same terms and subject to the same regulations as are provided in the sixth article of the treaty with the Omahas, so far as the same may be applicable. Any substantial improvements heretofore made by any Indian, and which he shall be compelled to abandon in consequence of this treaty, shall be valued under the direction of the President and payment made accordingly therefor.

ARTICLE 8
The annuities of the aforesaid tribes and bands shall not be taken to pay the debts of individuals.

ARTICLE 9
The said tribes and bands acknowledge their dependence on the Government of the United States, and promise to be friendly with all citizens thereof, and they pledge themselves to commit no depredations on the property of such citizens. Should any one or more of them violate this pledge, and the fact be satisfactorily proven before the agent, the property taken shall be returned, or in default thereof, of if injured or destroyed, compensation may be made by the Government out of their annuities. Nor will they make war on any other tribe except in self-defence, but will submit all matters of difference between them and the other Indians to the

Government of the United States or its agent for decision, and abide thereby. And if any of the said Indians commit depredations on other Indians within the Territory the same rule shall prevail as that prescribed in this article in cases of depredations against citizens. And the said tribes agree not to shelter or conceal offenders against the laws of the United States, but to deliver them up to the authorities for trial.

ARTICLE 10
The above tribes and bands are desirous to exclude from their reservations the use of ardent spirits, and to prevent their people from drinking the same, and therefore it is provided that any Indian belonging to said tribe who is guilty of bringing liquor into said reservations, or who drinks liquor, may have his or her proportion of the annuities withheld from him or her for such time as the President may determine.

ARTICLE 11
The said tribes and bands agree to free all slaves now held by them and not to purchase or acquire others hereafter.

ARTICLE 12
The said tribes and bands further agree not to trade at Vancouver's Island or elsewhere out of the dominions of the United States, nor shall foreign Indians be permitted to reside in their reservations without consent of the superintendent or agent.

ARTICLE 13
To enable the said Indians to remove to and settle upon their aforesaid reservations, and to clear, fence, and break up a sufficient quantity of land for cultivation, the United States further agree to pay the sum of fifteen thousand dollars to be laid out and expended under the direction of the President and in such manner as he shall approve.

ARTICLE 14
The United States further agree to establish at the general agency for the district of Puget's Sound, within one year from the ratification hereof, and to support for a period of twenty years, an agricultural and industrial school, to be free to children of the said

tribes and bands in common with those of the other tribes of said district, and to provide the said school with a suitable instructor or instructors, and also to provide a smithy and carpenter's shop, and furnish them with the necessary tools, and employ a blacksmith, carpenter, and farmer for the like term of twenty years to instruct the Indians in their respective occupations. And the United States finally agree to employ a physician to reside at the said central agency, who shall furnish medicine and advice to their sick, and shall vaccinate them; the expenses of said school, shops, persons employed, and medical attendance to be defrayed by the United States, and not deducted from the annuities.

ARTICLE 15

This treaty shall be obligatory on the contracting parties as soon as the same shall be ratified by the President and Senate of the United States.
In testimony whereof, the said Isaac I. Stevens, governor and superintendent of Indian affairs, and the undersigned chiefs, headmen, and delegates of the aforesaid tribes and bands of Indians, have hereunto set their hands and seals, at the place and on the day and year hereinbefore written.

Issac I. Stevens, Governor and Superintendent. (L.S.)
Seattle, Chief of the Dwamish and Suquamish tribes, his x mark. (L. S.)
Pat-ka-nam, Chief of the Snoqualmoo, Snohomish and other tribes, his x mark. (L.S.) Chow-its-hoot, Chief of the Lummi and other tribes, his x mark. (L. S.)
Goliah, Chief of the Skagits and other allied tribes, his x mark. (L.S.)
Kwallattum, or General Pierce, Sub-chief of the Skagit tribe, his x mark. (L.S.)
S'hootst-hoot, Sub-chief of Snohomish, his x mark. (L.S.)
Snah-talc, or Bonaparte, Sub-chief of Snohomish, his x mark. (L.S.)
Squush-um, or The Smoke, Sub-chief of the Snoqualmoo, his x mark. (L.S.)
See-alla-pa-han, or The Priest, Sub-chief of Sk-tah-le-jum, his x mark. (L.S.)
He-uch-ka-nam, or George Bonaparte, Sub-chief of Snohomish,

his x mark. (L.S.)
Tse-nah-talc, or Joseph Bonaparte, Sub-chief of Snohomish, his x mark. (L.S.)
Ns'ski-oos, or Jackson, Sub-chief of Snohomish, his x mark. (L.S.)
Wats-ka-lah-tchie, or John Hobtsthoot, Sub-chief of Snohomish, his x mark. (L.S.)
Smeh-mai-hu, Sub-chief of Skai-wha-mish, his x mark. (L.S.)
Slat-eah-ka-nam, Sub-chief of Snoqualmoo, his x mark. (L.S.)
St'hau-ai, Sub-chief of Snoqualmoo, his x mark. (L.S.)
Lugs-ken, Sub-chief of Skai-wha-mish, his x mark. (L.S.)
S'heht-soolt, or Peter, Sub-chief of Snohomish, his x mark. (L.S.)
Do-queh-oo-satl, Snoqualmoo tribe, his x mark. (L.S.)
John Kanam, Snoqualmoo sub-chief, his x mark. (L.S.)
Klemsh-ka-nam, Snoqualmoo, his x mark. (L.S.)
Ts'huahntl, Dwa-mish sub-chief, his x mark. (L.S.)
Kwuss-ka-nam, or George Snatelum, Sen., Skagit tribe, his x mark. (L.S.)
Hel-mits, or George Snatelum, Skagit sub-chief, his x mark. (L.S.)
S'kwai-kwi, Skagit tribe, sub-chief, his x mark. (L.S.)
Seh-lek-qu, Sub-chief Lummi tribe, his x mark. (L.S.)
S'h'-cheh-oos, or General Washington, Sub-chief of Lummi tribe, his x mark. (L.S.)
Whai-lan-hu, or Davy Crockett, Sub-chief of Lummi tribe, his x mark. (L.S.)
She-ah-delt-hu, Sub-chief of Lummi tribe, his x mark. (L.S.)
Kwult-seh, Sub-chief of Lummi tribe, his x mark. (L.S.)
Kwull-et-hu, Lummi tribe, his x mark. (L.S.)
Kleh-kent-soot, Skagit tribe, his x mark. (L.S.)
Sohn-heh-ovs, Skagit tribe, his x mark. (L.S.)
S'deh-ap-kan, or General Warren, Skagit tribe, his x mark. (L.S.)
Chul-whil-tan, Sub-chief of Suquamish tribe, his x mark. (L.S.)
Ske-eh-tum, Skagit tribe, his x mark. (L.S.)
Patchkanam, or Dome, Skagit tribe, his x mark. (L.S.)
Sats-Kanam, Squin-ah-nush tribe, his x mark. (L.S.)
Sd-zo-mahtl, Kik-ial-lus band, his x mark. (L.S.)
Dahtl-de-min, Sub-chief of Sah-ku-meh-hu, his x mark. (L.S.)
Sd'zek-du-num, Me-sek-wi-guilse sub-chief, his x mark. (L.S.)
Now-a-chais, Sub-chief of Dwamish, his x mark. (L.S.)
Mis-lo-tche, or Wah-hehl-tchoo, Sub-chief of Suquamish, his x mark. (L.S.)

Sloo-noksh-tan, or Jim, Suquamish tribe, his x mark. (L.S.)
Moo-whah-lad-hu, or Jack, Suquamish tribe, his x mark. (L.S.)
Too-leh-plan, Suquamish tribe, his x mark. (L.S.)
Ha-seh-doo-an, or Keo-kuck, Dwamish tribe, his x mark. (L.S.)
Hoovilt-meh-tum, Sub-chief of Suquamish, his x mark. (L.S.)
We-ai-pah, Skaiwhamish tribe, his x mark. (L.S.)
S'ah-an-hu, or Hallam, Snohomish tribe, his x mark. (L.S.)
She-hope, or General Pierce, Skagit tribe, his x mark. (L.S.)
Hwn-lah-lakq, or Thomas Jefferson, Lummi tribe, his x mark. (L.S.)
Cht-simpt, Lummi tribe, his x mark. (L.S.)
Tse-sum-ten, Lummi tribe, his x mark. (L.S.)
Klt-hahl-ten, Lummi tribe, his x mark. (L.S.)
Kut-ta-kanam, or John, Lummi tribe, his x mark. (L.S.)
Ch-lah-ben, Noo-qua-cha-mish band, his x mark. (L.S.)
Noo-heh-oos, Snoqualmoo tribe, his x mark. (L.S.)
Hweh-uk, Snoqualmoo tribe, his x mark. (L.S.)
Peh-nus, Skai-whamish tribe, his x mark. (L.S.)
Yim-ka-dam, Snoqualmoo tribe, his x mark. (L.S.)
Twooi-as-kut, Skaiwhamish tribe, his x mark. (L.S.)
Luch-al-kanam, Snoqualmoo tribe, his x mark. (L.S.)
S'hoot-kanam, Snoqualmoo tribe, his x mark. (L.S.)
Sme-a-kanam, Snoqualmoo tribe, his x mark. (L.S.)
Sad-zis-keh, Snoqualmoo, his x mark. (L.S.)
Heh-mahl, Skaiwhamish band, his x mark. (L.S.)
Charley, Skagit tribe, his x mark. (L.S.)
Sampson, Skagit tribe, his x mark. (L.S.)
John Taylor, Snohomish tribe, his x mark. (L.S.)
Hatch-kwentum, Skagit tribe, his x mark. (L.S.)
Yo-i-kum, Skagit tribe, his x mark. (L.S.)
T'kwa-ma-han, Skagit tribe, his x mark. (L.S.)
Sto-dum-kan, Swinamish band, his x mark. (L.S.)
Be-lole, Swinamish band, his x mark. (L.S.)
D'zo-lole-gwam-hu, Skagit tribe, his x mark. (L.S.)
Steh-shail, William, Skaiwhamish band, his x mark. (L.S.)
Kel-kahl-tsoot, Swinamish tribe, his x mark. (L.S.)
Pat-sen, Skagit tribe, his x mark. (L.S.)
Pat-teh-us, Noo-wha-ah sub-chief, his x mark. (L.S.)
S'hoolk-ka-nam, Lummi sub-chief, his x mark. (L.S.)
Ch-lok-suts, Lummi sub-chief, his x mark. (L.S.)

Executed in the presence of us - -
M. T. Simmons, Indian agent.
C. H. Mason, Secretary of Washington Territory.
Benj. F. Shaw, Interpreter.
Chas. M. Hitchcock.
H. a. Goldsborough.
George Gibbs.
John H. Scranton.
Henry D. Cock.
S. S. Ford, jr.
Orrington Cushman.
Ellis Barnes.
R. S. Bailey.
S. M. Collins.
Lafayetee Balch.
E. S. Fowler.
J. H. Hall.
Rob't Davis.
S. Doc. 319, 58-2, vol 2 43

Treaty of Point No Point, 1855

Articles of agreement and convention made and concluded at Hahdskus, or Point no Point, Suquamiah Head, in the Territory of Washington, this twenty-sixth day of January, eighteen hundred and fifty-five, by Isaac I. Stevens, governor and superintendent of Indian affairs for the said Territory, on the part of the United States, and the undersigned chiefs, headmen, and delegates of the different villages of the S'Klallams, viz: Kah-tai, Squah-quaihtl, Tch-queen, Ste-tehtlum, Tsohkw, Yennis, Elh-wa, Pishtst, Hunnint, Klat-la-wash, and Oke-ho, and also of the Sko-ko-mish, To-an-hooch, and Chem-a-kum tribes, occupying certain lands on the Straits of Fuca and Hood's Canal, in the Territory of Washington, on behalf of said tribes, and duly authorized by them.

ARTICLE 1
The said tribes and bands of Indians hereby cede, relinquish, and convey to the United States all their right, title, and interest in and to the lands and country occupied by them, bounded and described as follows, viz: Commencing at the mouth of the Okeho River, on

the Straits of Fuca; thence southeastwardly along the westerly line of territory claimed by the Makah tribe of Indians to the summit of the Cascade Range; thence still southeastwardly and southerly along said summit to the head of the west branch of the Satsop River, down that branch to the main fork; thence eastwardly and following the line of lands heretofore ceded to the the United States by the Nisqually and other tribes and bands of Indians, to the summit of the Black Hills, and northeastwardly to the portage known as Wilkes' Portage; thence northeastwardly, and following the line of lands heretofore ceded to the United States by the Dwamish, Suquamish, and other tribes and bands of Indians, to Suquamish Head; thence northerly through Admiralty Inlet to the Straits of Fuca; thence westwardly through said straits to the place of beginning; including all the right, title, and interest of the said tribes and bands to any land in the Territory of Washington.

ARTICLE 2
There is, however, reserved for the present use and occupation of the said tribes and bands the following tract of land, viz: The amount of six sections, or three thousand eight hundred and forty acres, situated at the head of Hood's Canal, to be hereafter set apart, and so far as necessary, surveyed and marked out for their exclusive use; nor shall any white man be permitted to reside upon the same without permission of the said tribes and bands, and of the superintendent or agent; but, if necessary for the public convenience, roads may be run through the said reservation, the Indians being compensated for any damage thereby done them. It is, however, understood that should the President of the United States hereafter see fit to place upon the said reservation any other friendly tribe or band, to occupy the same in common with those above mentioned, he shall be at liberty to do so.

ARTICLE 3
The said tribes and bands agree to remove to and settle upon the said reservation within one year after the ratification of this treaty, or sooner if the means are furnished them. In the mean time, it shall be lawful for them to reside upon any lands not in the actual claim or occupation of citizens of the United States, and upon any land claimed or occupied, if with the permission of the owner.

ARTICLE 4

The right of taking fish at usual and accustomed grounds and stations is further secured to said Indians, in common with all citizens of the United States; and of erecting temporary houses for the purpose of curing; together with the privilege of hunting and gathering roots and berries on open and unclaimed lands. Provided, however, That they shall not take shell-fish from any beds staked or cultivated by citizens.

ARTICLE 5

In consideration of the above cession the United States agree to pay to the said tribes and bands the sum of sixty thousand dollars, in the following manner, that is to say: during the first year after the ratification hereof, six thousand dollars; for the next two years, five thousand dollars each year; for the next three years, four thousand dollars each year; for the next four years, three thousand dollars each year; for the next five years, two thousand four hundred dollars each year; and for the next five years, one thousand six hundred dollars each year. All which said sums of money shall be applied to the use and benefit of the said Indians under the direction of the President of the United States, who may from time to time determine at his discretion upon what beneficial objects to expend the same. And the superintendent of Indian affairs, or other proper officer, shall each year inform the President of the wishes of said Indians in respect thereto.

ARTICLE 6

To enable the said Indians to remove to and settle upon their aforesaid reservations, and to clear, fence, and break up a sufficient quantity of land for cultivation, the United States further agree to pay the sum of six thousand dollars, to be laid out and expended under the direction of the President, and in such manner as he shall approve.

ARTICLE 7

The President may hereafter, when in his opinion the interests of the Territory shall require, and the welfare of said Indians be promoted, remove them from said reservation to such other suitable place or places within said Territory as he may deem fit, on remunerating them for their improvements and the expenses of their removal; or may consolidate them with other friendly tribes or bands. And he may further, at his discretion, cause the whole or any portion of the lands hereby reserved, or of such other lands as may be selected in lieu thereof, to be surveyed into lots, and assign the same to such individuals or families as are willing to avail themselves of the privilege, and will locate thereon as a permanent home, on the same terms and subject to the same regulations as are provided in the sixth article of the treaty with the Omahas, so far as the same may be applicable. Any substantial improvements heretofore made by any Indians, and which he shall be compelled to abandon in consequence of this treaty, shall be valued under the direction of the President, and payment made therefor accordingly.

ARTICLE 8
The annuities of the aforesaid tribes and bands shall not be taken to pay the debts of individuals.

ARTICLE 9
The said tribes and bands acknowledge their dependence on the Government of the United States, and promise to be friendly with all citizens thereof; and they pledge themselves to commit no depredations on the property of such citizens. And should any one or more of them violate this pledge, and the fact be satisfactorily proven before the agent, the property taken shall be returned, or in default thereof, or if injured or destroyed, compensation may be made by the Government out of their annuities. Nor will they make war on any other tribe, except in self-defence, but will submit all matters of difference between them and other Indians to the Government of the United States, or its agent, for decision, and abide thereby. And if any of the said Indians commit any depredations on any other Indians within the Territory, the same rule shall prevail as that prescribed in this article in cases of depredations against citizens. And the said tribes agree not to shelter or conceal offenders against the United States, but to deliver them up for trial by the authorities.

ARTICLE 10
The above tribes and bands are desirous to exclude from their reservation the use of ardent spirits, and to prevent their people from drinking the same, and therefore it is provided that any Indian

belonging thereto who shall be guilty of bringing liquor into said reservation, or who drinks liquor, may have his or her proportion of the annuities withheld from him or her for such time as the President may determine.

ARTICLE 11
The United States further agree to establish at the general agency for the district of Puget's Sound, within one year from the ratification hereof, and to support for the period of twenty years, an agricultural and industrial school, to be free to children of the said tribes and bands in common with those of the other tribes of said district, and to provide a smithy and carpenter's shop, and furnish them with the necessary tools, and employ a blacksmith, carpenter, and farmer for the term of twenty years, to instruct the Indians in their respective occupations. And the United States further agree to employ a physician to reside at the said central agency, who shall furnish medicine and advice to the sick, and shall vaccinate them; the expenses of the said school, shops, persons employed, and medical attendance to be defrayed by the United States, and not deducted from the annuities.

ARTICLE 12
The said tribes and bands agree to free all slaves now held by them, and not to purchase or acquire others hereafter.

ARTICLE 13

The said tribes and bands finally agree not to trade at Vancouver's Island, or elsewhere out of the dominions of the United States, nor shall foreign Indians be permitted to reside in their reservations without consent of the superintendent or agent.

ARTICLE 14
This treaty shall be obligatory on the contracting parties as soon as the same shall be ratified by the President of the United States.

In testimony whereof, the said Isaac I. Stevens, governor and superintendent of Indian affairs, and the undersigned chiefs, headmen, and delegates of the aforesaid tribes and bands of

Indians have hereunto set their hands and seals at the place and on the day and year herebefore written.

Isaac I. Stevens, governor and superintendent. (L.S.)
Chits-a-mah-han, the Duke of York, Chief of the S'klallams, his x mark. (L.S.)
Dah-whil-luk, Chief of the Sko-ko-mish, his x mark. (L.S.)
Kul-kah-han, or General Pierce, Chief of the Chem-a-kum, his x mark. (L.S.)
Hool-hole-tan, or Jim, Sko-ko-mish sub-chief, his x mark. (L.S.)
Sai-a-kade, or Frank, Sko-ko-mish sub-chief, his x mark. (L.S.)
Loo-gweh-oos, or George, Sko-ko-mish sub-chief, his x mark. (L.S.)
E-dagh-tan, or Tom, Sko-ko-mish sub-chief, his x mark. (L.S.)
Kai-a-han, or Daniel Webster, Chem-a-kum sub-chief, his x mark. (L. S.)
Ets-sah-quat, Chem-a-kum sub-chief, his x mark. (L.S.)
Kleh-a-kunst, Chem-a-kum sub-chief, his x mark. (L.S.)
He-atl, Duke of Clarence, S'klallam sub-chief, his x mark. (L.S.)
Lach-ka-nam, or Lord Nelson, S'klallam sub-chief, his x mark. (L. S.)
Tchotest, S'klallam sub-chief, his x mark. (L.S.)
Hoot-ote St, or General Lane, S'klallam sub-chief, his x mark. (L. S.)
To-totesh, S'klallam sub-chief, his x mark. (L.S.)
Hah-kwja-mihl, S'klallam sub-chief, his x mark. (L.S.)
Skai-se-ee, or Mr. Newman, S'klallam sub-chief, his x mark. (L.S.)
Kahs-sahs-a-matl, S'klallam sub-chief, his x mark. (L.S.)
S'hote-ch-stan, S'klallam sub-chief, his x mark. (L.S.)
Lah-st, or Tom, S'klallam sub-chief, his x mark. (L.S.)
Tuls-met-tum, Lord Jim, S'klallam sub-chief, his x mark. (L.S.)
Yaht-le-min, or General Taylor, S'klallam sub-chief, his x mark. (L.S.)
Kla-koisht, or Captain, S'klallam sub-chief, his x mark. (L.S.)
Sna-talc, or General Scott, S'klallam sub-chief, his x mark. (L.S.)
Tseh-a-take, or Tom Benton, S'klallam sub-chief, his x mark. (L.S.)
Yah-kwi-e-nook, or General Gaines, S'klallam sub-chief, his x mark. (L.S.)
Kai-at-lah, or General Lane, Jr., S'klallam sub-chief, his x mark.

(L.S.)
Captain Jack, S'klallam sub-chief, his x mark. (L.S.)
He-ach-kate, S'klallam sub-chief, his x mark. (L.S.)
T'soh-as-hau, or General Harrison, S'klallam sub-chief, his x mark. (L.S.)
Kwah-nalt-sote, S'klallam sub-chief, his x mark. (L.S.)
S'hoke-tan, S'klallam sub-chief, his x mark. (L.S.)
Paitl, S'klallam sub-chief, his x mark. (L.S.)
Wen-a-hap, S'klallam sub-chief, his x mark. (L.S.)
Klew-sum-ah, S'klallam sub-chief, his x mark. (L.S.)
Se-att-home-tau, S'klallam sub-chief, his x mark. (L.S.)
Tsat-sat-hoot, S'klallam tribe, his x mark. (L.S.)
Pe-an-ho, S'klallam tribe, his x mark. (L.S.)
Yi-ah-hum, or John Adams, S'klallam tribe, his x mark. (L.S.)
Ti-itch-stan, S'klallam tribe, his x mark. (L.S.)
Soo-yahntch, S'klallam tribe, his x mark. (L.S.)
Ttseh-a-take, S'klallam tribe, his x mark. (L.S.)
He-ats-at-soot, S'klallam tribe, his x mark. (L.S.)
Tow-oots-hoot, S'klallam tribe, his x mark. (L.S.)
Tsheh-ham, or General Pierce, S'klallam tribe, his x mark. (L.S.)
Kwin-nas-sum, or George, S'klallam tribe, his x mark. (L.S.)
Hai-ahts, John, S'klallam tribe, his x mark. (L.S.)
Hai-otest, John, S'klallam tribe, his x mark. (L.S.)
Seh-win-num, S'klallam tribe, his x mark. (L.S.)
Yai-tst, or George, S'klallam tribe, his x mark. (L.S.)
He-pait, or John, S'klallam tribe, his x mark. (L.S.)
Slimm, or John, S'klallam tribe, his x mark. (L.S.)
T'klalt-soot, or Jack, S'klallam tribe, his x mark. (L.S.)
S'tai-tan, or Sam, S'klallam tribe, his x mark. (L.S.)
Hut-tets-oot, S'klallam tribe, his x mark. (L.S.)
How-a-owl, S'klallam tribe, his x mark. (L.S.)

Executed in the presence of us - -
M. T. Simmons,
C. H. Mason, secretary Washington Territory,
Benj. F. Shaw, interpreter,
John H. Scranton,
Josiah P. Keller,
C. M. Hitchcock, M.D.,
A. B. Gove,

H. A. Goldsborough,
B. J. Madison,
F. A. Rowe,
Jas. M. Hunt,
George Gibbs, secretary,
John J. Reilly,
Robt. Davis,
S. S. Ford, Jr.,
H. D. Cock,
Orrington Cushman,
J. Conklin.
Ratified Mar. 8, 1859. Proclaimed Apr. 29, 1859.

Treaty of Neah Bay, 1855

Articles of agreement and convention, made and concluded at Neah Bay, in the Territory of Washington, this thirty-first day of January, in the year eighteen hundred and fifty-five, by Isaac I. Stevens, governor and superintendent of Indian affairs for the said Territory, on the part of the United States, and the undersigned chiefs, head-men, and delegates of the several villages of the Makah tribe of Indians, viz: Neah Waatch, Tsoo-Yess, and Osett, occupying the country around Cape Classett or Flattery, on behalf of the said tribe and duly authorized by the same.

ARTICLE 1
The said tribe hereby cedes, relinquishes, and conveys to the United States all their right, title, and interest in and to the lands and country occupied by it, bounded and described as follows, viz: Commencing at the mouth of the Oke-ho River, on the Straits of Fuca; thence running westwardly with said straits to Cape Classett or Flattery; thence southwardly along the coast to Osett, or the Lower Cape Flattery; thence eastwardly along the line of lands occupied by he Kwe-deh-tut or Kwill-eh-yute tribe of Indians, to the summit of the coast-range of mountains, and thence northwardly along the line of lands lately ceded to the United States by the S'Klallam tribe to the place of beginning, including all the islands lying off the same on the straits and coast.

ARTICLE 2

There is, however, reserved for the present use and occupation of the said tribe the following tract of land, viz:Commencing on the beach at the mouth of a small brook running into Neah Bay next to the site of the old Spanish fort; thence along the shore round Cape Classett or Flattery, to the mouth of another small stream running into the bay on the south side of said cape, a little above the Waatch village; thence following said brook to its source; thence in a straight line to the source of the first-mentioned brook, and thence following the same down to the place of beginning; which said tract shall be set apart, and so far as necessary surveyed and marked out for their exclusive use; nor shall any white man be permitted to reside upon the same without permission of the said tribe and of the superintendent or agent; but if necessary for the public convenience, roads may be run through the said reservation, the Indians being compensated for any damage thereby done them. It is, however, understood that should the President of the United States hereafter see fit to place upon the said reservation any other friendly tribe or band to occupy the same in common with those above mentioned, he shall be at liberty to do so.

ARTICLE 3

The said tribe agrees to remove to and settle upon the said reservation, if required so to do, within one year after the ratification of this treaty, or sooner, if the means are furnished them. In the mean time it shall be lawful for them to reside upon any land not in the actual claim and occupation of citizens of the United States, and upon any land claimed or occupied, if with the permission of the owner.

ARTICLE 4

The right of taking fish and of whaling or sealing at usual and accustomed grounds and stations is further secured to said Indians in common with all citizens of the United States, and of erecting temporary houses for the purpose of curing, together with the privilege of hunting and gathering roots and berries on open and unclaimed lands: Provided, however, That they shall not take shellfish from any beds staked or cultivated by citizens.

ARTICLE 5

In consideration of the above cession the United States agree to pay to the said tribe the sum of thirty thousand dollars, in the following manner, that is to say: During the first year after the ratification hereof, three thousand dollars; for the next two years, twenty-five hundred dollars each year; for the next three years, two thousand dollars each year; for the next four years, one thousand five hundred dollars each year; and for the next ten years, one thousand dollars each year; all which said sums of money shall be applied to the use and benefit of the said Indians, under the direction of the President of the United States, who may from time to time determine at his discretion upon what beneficial objects to expend the same. And the superintendent of Indian affairs, or other proper officer, shall each year inform the President of the wishes of said Indians in respect thereto.

ARTICLE 6

To enable the said Indians to remove to and settle upon their aforesaid reservation, and to clear, fence, and break up a sufficient quantity of land for cultivation, the United States further agree to pay the sum of three thousand dollars, to be laid out and expended under the direction of the President, and in such manner as he shall approve. And any substantial improvements heretofore made by any individual Indian, and which he may be compelled to abandon in consequence of this treaty, shall be valued under the direction of the President and payment made therefor accordingly.

ARTICLE 7

The President may hereafter, when in his opinion the interests of the Territory shall require, and the welfare of said Indians be promoted thereby, remove them from said reservation to such suitable place or places within said Territory as he may deem fit, on remunerating them for their improvements and the expenses of their removal, or may consolidate them with other friendly tribes or bands; and he may further, at his discretion, cause the whole, or any portion of the lands hereby reserved, or such other land as may be selected in lieu thereof, to be surveyed into lots, and assign the same to such individuals or families as are willing to avail themselves of the privilege, and will locate thereon as a permanent home, on the same terms and subject to the same regulations as are provided in the sixth article of the treaty with the Omahas, so far as the same may be practicable.

ARTICLE 8

The annuities of the aforesaid tribe shall not be taken to pay the debts of individuals.

ARTICLE 9

The said Indians acknowledge their dependence on the Government of the United States, and promise to be friendly with all citizens thereof, and they pledge themselves to commit no depredations on the property of such citizens. And should any one or more of them violate this pledge, and the fact be satisfactorily proven before the agent, the property taken shall be returned, or in default thereof, or if injured or destroyed, compensation may be made by the Government out of their annuities. Nor will they make war on any other tribe except in self-defence, but will submit all matters of difference between them and other Indians to the Government of the United States or its agent for decision and abide thereby. And if any of the said Indians commit any depredations on any other Indians within the Territory, the same rule shall prevail as that prescribed in this article in case of depredations against citizens. And the said tribe agrees not to shelter or conceal offenders against the United States, but to deliver up the same for trial by the authorities.

ARTICLE 10

The above tribe is desirous to exclude from its reservation the use of ardent spirits, and to prevent its people from drinking the same, and therefore it is provided that any Indian belonging thereto who shall be guilty of bringing liquor into said reservation, or who drinks liquor, may have his or her proportion of the annuities withheld from him or her for such time as the President may determine

ARTICLE 11

The United States further agree to establish at the general agency for the district of Puget's Sound, within one year from the ratification hereof, and to support for the period of twenty years, an agricultural and industrial school, to be free to children of the said tribe in common with those of the other tribes of said district and to provide a smithy and carpenter's shop, and furnish them with the necessary tools and employ a blacksmith, carpenter and farmer for the like term to instruct the Indians in their respective occupations. Provided, however, That should it be deemed expedient a separate school may be established for the benefit of said tribe and such others as may be associated with it, and the like persons employed for the same purposes at some other suitable place. And the United States further agree to employ a physician to reside at the said central agency, or at such other school should one be established, who shall furnish medicine and advice to the sick, and shall vaccinate them; the expenses of the said school, shops, persons employed, and medical attendance to be defrayed by the United States and not deducted from the annuities.

ARTICLE 12
The said tribe agrees to free all slaves now held by its people, and not to purchase or acquire others hereafter.

ARTICLE 13
The said tribe finally agrees not to trade at Vancouver's Island or elsewhere out of the dominions of the United States, nor shall foreign Indians be permitted to reside in its reservation without consent of the superintendent or agent.

ARTICLE 14
This treaty shall be obligatory on the contracting parties as soon as the same shall be ratified by the President of the United States.

In testimony whereof, the said Isaac I. Stevens, governor and superintendent of Indian affairs, and the undersigned, chiefs, headmen and delegates of the tribe aforesaid have hereunto set their hands and seals at the place and on the day and year hereinbefore written.

Isaac I. Stevens, governor and superintendent. (L.S.)
Tse-kauwtl, head chief of the Makah tribe, his x mark. (L.S.)
Kal-chote, subchief of the Makahs, his x mark. (L.S.)
Tah-a-howtl, subchief of the Makahs, his x mark. (L.S.)
Kah-bach-sat, subchief of the Makahs, his x mark. (L.S.)

Kets-kus-sum, subchief of the Makahs, his x mark. (L.S.)
Haatse, subchief of the Makahs, his x mark. (L.S.)
Keh-chook, subchief of the Makahs, his x mark. (L.S.)
It-an-da-ha, subchief of the Makahs, his x mark. (L.S.)
Klah-pe-an-hie, or Andrew Jackson, subchief of the Makahs, his x mark. (L.S.)
Tsal-ab-oos, or Peter, Neah village, his x mark. (L.S.)
Tahola, Neah village, his x mark. (L.S.)
Kleht-li-quat-stl, Waatch village, his x mark. (L.S.)
Too-whaii-tan, Waatch village, his x mark. (L.S.)
Tahts-kin, Neah village, his x mark. (L.S.)
Nenchoop, Neah village, his x mark. (L.S.)
Ah-de-ak-too-ah, Osett village, his x mark. (L.S.)
William, Neah village, his x mark. (L.S.)
Wak-kep-tup, Waatch village, his x mark. (L.S.)
Klaht-te-di-yuke, Waatch village, his x mark. (L.S.)
Oobick, Waatch village, his x mark. (L.S.)
Bich-took, Waatch village, his x mark. (L.S.)
Baht-se-ditl, Neah village, his x mark. (L.S.)
Wack-shie, Neah village, his x mark. (L.S.)
Hah-yo-hwa, Waatch village, his x mark. (L.S.)
Daht-leek, or Mines, Osett village, his x mark. (L.S.)
Pah-hat, Neah village, his x mark. (L.S.)
Pai-yeh, Osett village, his x mark. (L.S.)
Tsah-weh-sup, Neah village, his x mark. (L.S.)
Al-is-kah, Osett village, his x mark. (L.S.)
Kwe-tow'tl, Neah village, his x mark. (L.S.)
Kaht-saht-wha, Neah village, his x mark. (L.S.)
Tchoo-quut-lah, or Yes Sir, Neah village, his x mark. (L.S.)
Klatts-ow-sehp, Neah village, his x mark. (L.S.)
Kai-kl-chis-sum, Neah village, his x mark. (L.S.)
Kah-kwt-lit-ha, Waatch village, his x mark. (L.S.)
He-dah-titl, Neah village, his x mark. (L.S.)
Sah-dit-le-uad, Waatch village, his x mark. (L.S.)
Klah-ku-pihl, Tsoo-yess village, his x mark. (L.S.)
Billuk-whtl, Tsoo-yess village, his x mark. (L.S.)
Kwah-too-qualh, Tsoo-yess village, his x mark. (L.S.)
Yooch-boott, Tsoo-yess village, his x mark. (L.S.)
Swell, or Jeff. Davis. Neah village, his x mark. (L.S.)

Executed in the presence of us. The words "five hundred" being first interlined in the 5th article, and erasures made in the 8th and 9th articles.

M. T. Simmons, Indian agent.
George Gibbs, secretary.
B. F. Shaw, interpreter.
C. M. Hitchcock, M. D.
E. S. Fowler,
Orrington Cushman.
Robt. Davis.
Ratified Mar. 8, 1859. Proclaimed Apr. 18, 1859.

Treaty of Yakama, 1855

ARTICLE 1
The aforesaid confederated tribes and bands of Indians hereby cede, relinquish, and convey to the United States all their right, title, and interest in and to the lands and country occupied and claimed by them, and bounded and described as follows, to wit: Commencing at Mount Rainier, thence northerly along the main ridge of the Cascade Mountains to the point where the northern tributaries of Lake Che-lan and the southern tributaries of the Methow River have their rise; thence southeasterly on the divide between the waters of Lake Che-lan and the Methow River to the Columbia River; thence, crossing the Columbia on a true east course, to a point whose longitude is one hundred and nineteen degrees and ten minutes, (119 10',) which two latter lines separate the above confederated tribes and bands from the Oakinakane tribe of Indians; thence in a true south course to the forty-seventh (47) parallel of latitude; thence east on said parallel to the main Palouse River, which two latter lines of boundary separate the above confederated tribes and bands from the Spokanes; thence down the Palouse River to its junction with the Moh-hah-ne-she, or southern tributary of the same; thence in a southeasterly direction, to the Snake River, at the mouth of the Tucannon River, separating the above confederated tribes from the Nez Perce tribe of Indians; thence down the Snake River to its junction with the Columbia River; thence up the Columbia River to the "White Banks" below the Priest's Rapids; thence westerly to a lake called "La Lac;"

thence southerly to a point on the Yakama River called Toh-mah-luke; thence, in a southwesterly direction, to the Columbia River, at the western extremity of the "Big Island," between the mouths of the Umatilla River and Butler Creek; all which latter boundaries separate the above confederated tribes and bands from the Walla-Walla Cayuse, and Umatilla tribes and bands of Indians; thence down the Columbia River to midway between the mouths of White Salmon and Wind Rivers; thence along the divide between said rivers to the main ridge of the Cascade Mountains; and thence along said ridge to the place of beginning.

ARTICLE 2

There is, however, reserved, from the lands above ceded for the use and occupation of the aforesaid confederated tribes and bands of Indians, the tract of land included within the following boundaries, to wit: Commencing on the Yakama River, at the mouth of the Attah-nam River; thence westerly along said Attah-nam River to the forks; thence along the southerly tributary to the Cascade Mountains; thence southerly along the main ridge of said mountains, passing south and east of Mount Adams, to the spur whence flows the waters of the Klickatat and Pisco Rivers; thence down said spur to the divide between the waters of said rivers; thence along said divide to the divide separating the waters of the Satass River from those flowing into the Columbia River; thence along said divide to the main Yakama, eight miles below the mouth of the Satass River; and thence up the Yakama River to the place of beginning. All which tract shall be set apart and, so far as necessary, surveyed and marked out, for the exclusive use and benefit of said confederated tribes and bands of Indians, as an Indian reservation, nor shall any white man, excepting those in the employment of the Indian Department, be permitted to reside upon the said reservation without permission of the tribe and the superintendent and agent. And the said confederated tribes and bands agree to remove to, and settle upon, the same, within one year after the ratification of this treaty. In the meantime it shall be lawful for them to reside upon any ground not in the actual claim and occupation of citizens of the United States; and upon any ground claimed or occupied, if with the permission of the owner or claimant. Guaranteeing, however, the right to all citizens of the United States to enter upon and occupy as settlers any lands not actually occupied and cultivated by said Indians at this time, and not included in the reservation above named. And provided, That any substantial improvements heretofore made by any Indian, such as fields enclosed and cultivated and houses erected upon the lands hereby ceded, and which he may be compelled to abandon in consequence of this treaty, shall be valued, under the direction of the President of the United States, and payment made therefor in money; or improvements of an equal value made for said Indian upon the reservation. And no Indian will be required to abandon the improvements aforesaid, now occupied by him, until their value in money, or improvements of an equal value shall be furnished him as aforesaid.

ARTICLE 3
And provided, that, if necessary for the public convenience, roads may be run through the said reservation; and on the other hand, the right of way, with free access from the same to the nearest public highway, is secured to them; as also the right, in common with citizens of the United States, to travel upon all public highways. The exclusive right of taking fish in all the streams, where running through or bordering said reservation, is further secured to said confederated tribes and bands of Indians, as also the right of taking fish at all usual and accustomed places, in common with the citizens of the Territory, and of erecting temporary buildings for curing them: together with the privilege of hunting, gathering roots and berries, and pasturing their horses and cattle upon open and unclaimed land.

ARTICLE 4
In consideration of the above cession, the United States agree to pay to the said confederated tribes and bands of Indians, in addition to the goods and provisions distributed to them at the time of signing this treaty, the sum of two hundred thousand dollars, in the following manner, that is to say: Sixty thousand dollars, to be expended under the direction of the President of the United States, the first year after the ratification of this treaty, in providing for their removal to the reservation, breaking up and fencing farms, building houses for them, supplying them with provisions and a suitable outfit, and for such other objects as he may deem necessary, and the remainder in annuities, as follows: For the first

five years after the ratification of the treaty, ten thousand dollars each year, commencing September first, 1856; for the next five years, eight thousand dollars each year; for the next five years, six thousand dollars per year; and for the next five years, four thousand dollars per year. All which sums of money shall be applied to the use and benefit of said Indians, under the direction of the President of the United States, who may from time to time determine, at his discretion, upon what beneficial objects to expend the same for them. And the superintendent of Indian affairs, or other proper officer, shall each year inform the President of the wishes of the Indians in relation thereto.

ARTICLE 5
The United States further agree to establish at suitable points within said reservation, within one year after the ratification hereof, two schools, erecting the necessary buildings, keeping them in repair, and providing them with furniture, books, and stationery; one of which shall be an agricultural and industrial school, to be located at the agency, and to be free to the children of the said confederated tribes and bands of Indians, and to employ one superintendent of teaching and two teachers; to build two blacksmiths' shops, to one of which shall be attached a tin-shop, and to the other a gunsmith's shop; one carpenters shop, one wagon and plough makeers shop, and to keep the same in repair and furnished with the necessary tools; to employ one superintendent of farming and two farmers, two blacksmiths, one tinner, one gunsmith, one carpenter, one wagon and plough maker, for the instruction of the Indians in trade and to assist them in the same; to erect one saw-mill and flouring-mill, keeping the same in repair and furnished with the neccessary tools and fixtures; to erect a hospital, keeping the same in repair and provided with the necessary medicines and furniture, and to employ a physician, and to erect, keep in repair, and provided with the necessary furniture, the building required for the accomodation of the said employees. The said buildings and establishments to be maintained and kept in repair as aforesaid, and the employees to be kept in service for the period of twenty years. And in view of the fact that the head chief of the said confederated tribes and bands of Indians is expected, and will be called upon to perform many services of a public character, occupying much of his time, the United States further

agree to pay to the said confederated tribes and bands of Indians five hundred dollars per year, for the term of twenty years after the ratification hereof, as a salary for such person as the said confederated tribes and bands of Indians may select to be their head chief, to build for him at a suitable point on the reservation a comfortable house, and properly furnish the same, and to plough and fence ten acres of land. The said salary to be paid to, and the said house to be occupied by, such head chief so long he may continue to hold that office. And it is distinctly understood and agreed that at the time of the conclusion of this treaty Kamaiakum is the duly elected and authorized head chief of the confederated tribes and bands aforesaid, styled the Yakama Nation, and is recognized as such by them and by the commissioners on the part of the United States holding this treaty; and all the expenditures and expenses contemplated in this article of this treaty shall be defrayed by the United States, and shall not be deducted from the annuities agreed to be paid to said confederated tribes and band of Indians. Nor shall the cost of transporting the goods for the annuity payments be a charge upon the annuities, but shall be defrayed by the United States.

ARTICLE 6
The President may, from time to time, at his discretion, cause the whole or such portions of such reservation as he may think proper, to be surveyed into lots, and assign the same to such individuals or families of the said confederated tribes and bands of Indians as are willing to avail themselves of the privilege, and will locate on the same as a permanent home, on the same terms and subject to the same regulations as are provided in the sixth article of the treaty with the Omahas, so far as the same may be applicable.

ARTICLE 7
The annuities of the aforesaid confederated tribes and bands of Indians shall not be taken to pay the debts of individuals.

ARTICLE 8
The aforesaid confederated tribes and bands of Indians acknowledge their dependence upon the Government of the United States, and promise to be friendly with all citizens thereof, and pledge themselves to commit no depredations upon the property of

such citizens. And should any one or more of them violate this pledge, and the fact be satisfactorily proved before the agent, the property taken shall be returned, or in default thereof, or if injured or destroyed, compensation may be made by the Government out of the annuities. Nor will they make war upon any other tribe, except in self-defense, but will submit all matters of difference between them and other Indians to the Government of the United States or its agent for decision, and abide thereby. And if any of the said Indians commit depredations on any other Indians within the Territory of Washington or Oregon, the same rule shall prevail as that provided in this article in case of depredations against citizens. And the said confederated tribes and bands of Indians agree not to shelter or conceal offenders against the laws of the United States, but to deliver them up to the authorities for trial.

ARTICLE 9
The said confederated tribes and bands of Indians desire to exclude from their reservation the use of ardent spirits, and to prevent their people from drinking the same, and, therefore, it is provided that any Indian belonging to said confederated tribes and bands of Indians, who is guilty of bringing liquor into said reservation, or who drinks liquor, may have his or her annuities withheld from him or her for such time as the President may determine.

ARTICLE 10
And provided That there is also reserved and set apart from the lands ceded by this treaty, for the use and benefit of the aforesaid confederated tribes and bands, a tract of land not exceeding in quantity one township of six miles square, situated at the forks of the Pisquouse or Wenatshapam River, and known as the "Wenatshapam Fishery," which said reservation shall be surveyed and marked out whenever the President may direct, and be subject to the same provisions and restrictions as other Indian reservations.

ARTICLE 11
This treaty shall be obligatory, upon the contracting parties as soon as the same shall be ratified by the President and Senate of the United States. In testimony whereof, the said Isaac I. Stevens, governor and superintendent of Indian affairs for the Territory of Washington, and the undersigned head chief, chiefs, headmen, and

delegates of the aforesaid confederated tribes and bands of Indians have here unto set their hands and seals, at the place and on the day and year hereinbefore written.

ISAAC I. STEVENS, Governor and Superintendent. [L.S.]
Kamaiakun, his mark.
Wish-och-kmpits, his x mark.
Skloom, his x mark.
Koo-lat-toose, his x mark.
Owhi, his x mark.
Shee-ah-cotte, his x mark.
Te-cole-kun, his x mark.
Tuck-quille, his x mark.
La-hoom, his x mark.
Ka-loo-as, his x mark.
Me-ni-nock, his x mark.
Scha-noo-a, his x mark.
Elit Paliller, his x mark.
Sla-kish, his x mark.

Signed and sealed in the presence of-
James Doty, secretary of treaties,
Mie. Cles. Pandosy, O.M.T.,
Wm. C. McKay,
W. H. Tappan; sub Indian agent, W. T.,
C. Chirouse, O. M. T.,
Patrick McKenzie, interpreter,
A. D. Pamburn, interpreter,
Joel Palmer, superintendent Indian affairs, O.T.,
W. D. Biglow,
A. D. Pamburn, interpreter.

Treaty of Walla Walla, 1855

ARTICLE 1
The above-named confederated bands of Indians cede to the United States all their right, title, and claim to all and every part of the country claimed by them included in the following boundaries, to wit: Commencing at the mouth of the Tocannon River, in Washington Territory, running thence up said river to its source;

thence easterly along the summit of the Blue Mountains, and on the southern boundaries of the purchase made of the Nez Perces Indians, and easterly along that boundary to the western limits of the country claimed by the Shoshonees or Snake Indians; thence southerly along that boundary (being the waters of Powder River) to the source of Powder River, thence to the head-waters of Willow Creek, thence down Willow Creek to the Columbia River, thence up the channel of the Columbia River to the lower end of a large island below the mouth of Umatilla River, thence northerly to a point on the Yakama River, called Tomah-luke, thence to Le Lac, thence to the White Banks on the Columbia below Priest's Rapids, thence down the Columbia River to the junction of the Columbia and Snake Rivers, thence up the Snake River to the place of beginning: Provided, however, That so much of the country described above as is contained in the following boundaries shall be set apart as a residence for said Indians, which tract for the purposes contemplated shall be held and regarded as an Indian reservation; to wit: Commencing in the middle of the channel of Umatilla River opposite the mouth of Wild Horse Creek, thence up the middle of the channel of said creek to its source, thence southerly to a point in the Blue Mountains, known as Lee's Encampment, thence in a line to the head-waters of Howtome Creek, thence west to the divide between Howtome and Birch Creeks, thence northerly along said divide to a point due west of the southwest corner of William C. McKay's land-claim, thence east along his line to his southeast corner, thence in a line to the place of beginning; all of which tract shall be set apart and, so far as necessary, surveyed and marked out for their exclusive use; nor shall any white person be permitted to reside upon the same without permission of the agent and superintendent. The said tribes and bands
agree to remove to and settle upon the same within one year after the ratification of this treaty, without any additional expense to the Government other than is provided by this treaty, and until the expiration of the time specified, the said bands shall be permitted to occupy and reside upon the tracts now possessed by them, guaranteeing to all citizen(s) of the United States, the right to enter upon and occupy as settlers any lands not actually enclosed by said Indians: Provided, also, That the exclusive right of taking fish in the streams running through and bordering said reservation is

hereby secured to said Indians, and at all other usual and accustomed stations in common with citizens of the United States, and of erecting suitable buildings for curing the same; the privilege of hunting, gathering roots and berries and pasturing their stock on unclaimed lands in common with citizens, is also secured to them. And provided, also, That if any band or bands of Indians, residing in and claiming any portion or portions of the country described in this article, shall not accede to the terms of this treaty, then the bands becoming parties hereunto agree to reserve such part of the several and other payments herein named, as a consideration for the entire country described as aforesaid, as shall be in the proportion that their aggregate number may have to the whole number of Indians residing in and claiming the entire country aforesaid, as consideration and payment in full for the tracts in said country claimed by them. And provided, also, That when substantial improvements have been made by any member of the bands being parties to this treaty, who are compelled to abandon them in consequence of said treaty, (they) shall be valued under the direction of the President of the United States, and payment made therefor.

ARTICLE 2

In consideration of and payment for the country hereby ceded, the United States agree to pay the bands and tribes of Indians claiming territory and residing in said country, and who remove to and reside upon said reservation, the several sums of money following, to wit: eight thousand dollars per annum for the term of five years, commencing on the first day of September, 1856; six thousand dollars per annum for the term of five years next succeeding the first five; four thousand dollars per annum for the term of five years next succeeding the second five, and two thousand dollars per annum for the term of five years next succeeding the third five; all of which several sums of money shall be expended for the use and benefit of the confederated bands herein named, under the direction of the President of the United States, who may from time to time at his discretion, determine what proportion thereof shall be expended for such objects as in his judgment will promote their well-being, and advance them in civilization, for their moral improvement and education, for buildings, opening and fencing farms, breaking, land, purchasing teams, wagons, agricultural implements and seeds, for clothing, provision and tools, for medical purposes, providing mechanics and farmers, and for arms and ammunition.

ARTICLE 3
In addition to the articles advanced the Indians at the time of signing this treaty, the United States agree to expend the sum of fifty thousand dollars during the first and second years after its ratification, for the erection of buildings on the reservation, fencing and opening farms, for the purchase of teams, farming implements, clothing, and provisions, for medicines and tools, for the payment of employes, and for subsisting the Indians the first year after their removal.

ARTICLE 4
In addition to the consideration above specified, the United States agree to erect, at suitable points on the Reservation, one saw-mill, and one flouring-mill, a building suitable for a hospital, two school-houses, one blacksmith shop, one building for wagon and plough maker and one carpenter and joiner shop, one dwelling for each, two millers, one farmer, one superintendent of farming operations, two school-teachers, one blacksmith, one wagon and plough maker, one carpenter and joiner, to each of which the necessary out-buildings. To purchase and keep in repair for the term of twenty years all necessary mill fixtures and mechanical tools, medicines and hospital stores, books and stationery for schools, and furniture for employes.
The United States further engage to secure and pay for the services and subsistence, for the term of twenty years, (of) one superintendent of farming operations, one farmer, one blacksmith, one wagon and plough maker, one carpenter and joiner, one physician, and two school-teachers.

ARTICLE 5
The United States further engage to build for the head chiefs of the Walla-Walla, Cayuse, and Umatilla bands each one dwelling-house, and to plough and fence ten acres of land for each, and to pay to each five hundred dollars per annum in cash for the term of twenty years. The first payment to the Walla-Walla chief to commence upon the signing of this treaty. To give to the Walla-

Walla chief three yoke of oxen, three yokes and four chains, one wagon, two ploughs, twelve hoes, twelve axes, two shovels, and one saddle and bridle, one set of wagon-harness, and one set of plough-harness, within three months after the signing of this treaty. To build for the son of Pio-pio-mox-mox one dwelling-house, and plough and fence five acres of land, and to give him a salary for twenty years, one hundred dollars in cash per annum, commencing September first, eighteen hundred and fifty-six. The improvement named in this section to be completed as soon after the ratification of this treaty as possible.

It is further stipulated that Pio-pio-mox-mox is secured for the term of five years, the right to build and occupy a house at or near the mouth of Yakama River, to be used as a trading-post in the sale of his bands of wild cattle ranging in that district: And provided, also, That in consequence of the immigrant wagon-road from Grand Round to

Umatilla, passing through the reservation herein specified, thus leading to turmoils and disputes between Indians and immigrants, and as it is known that a more desirable and practicable route may be had to the south of the present road, that a sum not exceeding ten thousand dollars shall be expended in locating and opening a wagon-road from

Powder River or Grand Round, so as to reach the plain at the western base of the Blue Mountain, south of the southern limits of said reservation.

ARTICLE 6

The President may, from time to time at his discretion cause the whole or such portion as he may think proper, of the tract that may now or hereafter be set apart as a permanent home for those Indians, to be surveyed into lots and assigned to such Indians of the confederated bands as may wish to enjoy the privilege, and locate thereon permanently, to a single person over twenty-one years of age, forty acres, to a family of two persons, sixty acres, to a family of three and not exceeding five, eighty acres; to a family of six persons and not exceeding ten, one hundred and twenty acres; and to each family over ten in number, twenty acres to each additional three members; and the President may provide for such rules and regulations as will secure to the family in case of the death of the head thereof, the possession and enjoyment of such permanent home and improvement thereon; and he may at any time, at his discretion, after such person or family has made location on the land assigned as a permanent home, issue a patent to such person or family for such assigned land, conditioned that the tract shall not be aliened or leased for a longer term than two years, and shall be exempt from levy, sale, or forfeiture, which condition shall continue in force until a State constitution, embracing such land within its limits, shall have been formed and the legislature of the State shall remove the restriction: Provided, however, That no State legislature shall remove the restriction herein provided for without the consent of Congress: And provided, also, That if any person or family, shall at any time, neglect or refuse to occupy or till a portion of the land assigned and on which they have located, or shall roam from place to place, indicating a desire to abandon his home, the President may if the patent shall have been issued, cancel the assignment, and may also withhold from such person or family their portion of the annuities or other money due them, until they shall have returned to such permanent home, and resumed the pursuits of industry, and in default of their return the tract may be declared abandoned, and thereafter assigned to some other person or family of Indians residing on said reservatio: And provided, also, That the head chiefs of the three principal bands, to wit, Pio-pio-mox-mox, Weyatenatemany, and Wenap-snoot, shall be secured in a tract of at least one hundred and sixty acres of land.

ARTICLE 7
The annuities of the Indians shall not be taken to pay the debts of individuals.

ARTICLE 8
The confederated bands acknowledge their dependence on the Government of the United States and promise to be friendly with all the citizens thereof, and pledge themselves to commit no depredation on the property of such citizens, and should any one or more of the Indians violate this pledge, and the fact be satisfactorily proven before the agent, the property taken shall be returned, or in default thereof, or if injured or destroyed, compensation may be made by the Government out of their annuities; nor will they make war on any other tribe of Indians

except in self-defense, but submit all matter of difference between them and other Indians, to the Government of the United States or its agents for decision, and abide thereby; and if any of the said Indians commit any depredations on other Indians, the same rule shall prevail as that prescribed in the article in case of depredations against citizens. Said Indians further engage to submit to and observe all laws, rules, and regulations which may be prescribed by the United States for the government of said Indians.

ARTICLE 9

In order to prevent the evils of intemperance among said Indians, it is hereby provided that if any one of them shall drink liquor, or procure it for others to drink, (such one) may have his or her proportion of the annuities withheld from him or her for such time as the President may determine.

ARTICLE 10

The said confederated bands agree that, whenever in the opinion of the President of the United States the public interest may require it, that all roads highways and railroads shall have the right of way through the reservation herein designated or which may at any time hereafter be set apart as a reservation for said Indians.

ARTICLE 11

This treaty shall be obligatory on the contracting parties as soon as the same shall be ratified by the President and
Senate of the United States.
In testimony whereof, the said I. I. Stevens and Joel Palmer, on the part of the United States, and the undersigned chiefs, headmen, and delegates of the said confederated bands, have hereunto set their hands and seals, this ninth day of June, eighteen hundred and fifty-five.

Isaac I. Stevens, (L.S.)
Governor and Superintendent Washington Territory.
Joel Palmer, (L.S.)
Superintendent Indian Affairs, O.T.
Pio-pio-mox-mox, his x mark, head chief of Walla-Wallas. (L.S.)
Meani-teat or Pierre, his x mark. (L.S.)
Weyatenatemany, his x mark, head chief of Cayuses. (L.S.)

Wenap-snoot, his x mark, head chief of Umatilla. (L.S.)
Kamaspello, his x mark. (L.S.)
Steachus, his x mark. (L.S.)
Howlish-wampo, his x mark. (L.S.)
Five Crows, his x mark. (L.S.)
Stocheania, his x mark. (L.S.)
Mu-howlish, his x mark. (L.S.)
Lin-tin-met-cheania, his x mark. (L.S.)
Petamyo-mox-mox, his x mark. (L.S.)
Watash-te-waty, his x mark. (L.S.)
She-yam-na-kon, his x mark. (L.S.)
Qua-chim, his x mark. (L.S.)
Te-walca-temany, his x mark. (L.S.)
Keantoan, his x mark. (L.S.)
U-wait-quaick, his x mark. (L.S.)
Tilch-a-waix, his x mark. (L.S.)
La-ta-chin, his x mark. (L.S.)
Kacho-rolich, his x mark. (L.S.)
Kanocey, his x mark. (L.S.)
Som-na-howlish, his x mark. (L.S.)
Ta-we-way, his x mark. (L.S.)
Ha-hats-me-cheat-pus, his x mark. (L.S.)
Pe-na-cheanit, his x mark. (L.S.)
Ha-yo-ma-kin, his x mark. (L.S.)
Ya-ca-lox, his x mark. (L.S.)
Na-kas, his x mark. (L.S.)
Stop-cha-yeou, his x mark. (L.S.)
He-yeau-she-keaut, his x mark. (L.S.)
Sha-wa-way, his x mark. (L.S.)
Tam-cha-key, his x mark. (L.S.)
Te-na-we-na-cha, his x mark. (L.S.)
Johnson, his x mark. (L.S.)
Whe-la-chey, his x mark. (L.S.)

Signed in the presence of - -
James Doty, secretary treaties.
Wm. C. McKay, secretary treaties.
C. Chirouse, O.M.I.
A. D. Pamburn, interpreter.
John Whitford, his x mark, interpreter.

Mathew Dofa, his x mark, interpreter.
William Craig, interpreter.
James Coxey, his x mark, interpreter.
Patrick McKenzie, interpreter.
Arch. Gracie, jr., brevet second lieutenant, Fourth Infantry.
R. R. Thompson, Indian agent.
R. B. Metcalfe, Indian sub-agent.
Ratified Mar. 8, 1859.
Proclaimed Apr. 11, 1859.

Treaty of Quinault, 1856

ARTICLE 1
The said tribes and bands hereby cede, relinquish, and convey to the United States all their right, title, and interest in and to the lands and country occupied by them, bounded and described as follows: Commencing at a point on the Pacific coast, which is the southwest corner of the lands lately ceded by the Makah tribe of Indians to the United States, and running easterly with and along the southern boundary of the said Makah tribe to the middle of the coast range of mountains; thence southerly with said range of mountains to their intersection with the dividing ridge between the chehalis and Quiniatl Rivers; thence westerly with said ridge to the Pacific coast; thence northerly along said coast to the place of beginning.

ARTICLE 2
There shall, however, be reserved, for the use and occupation of the tribes and bands aforesaid, a tract or tracts of land sufficient for their wants within the Territory of Washington, to be selected by the President of the United States, and hereafter surveyed or located and set apart for their exclusive use, and no white man shall be permitted to reside thereon without permission of the tribe and of the superintendent of Indian affairs or Indian agent. And the said tribes and bands agree to remove to and settle upon the same within one year after the ratification of this treaty, or sooner if the means are furnished them. In the meantime it shall be lawful for them to reside upon any lands not in the actual claim and occupation of citizens of the United States, and upon any lands claimed or occupied, if with the permission of the owner or

claimant. If necessary for the public convenience, roads may be run through said reservation, on compensation being made for any damage sustained thereby.

ARTICLE 3
The right of taking fish at all usual and accustomed grounds and stations is secured to said Indians in common with all citizens of the Territory, and of erecting temporary houses for the purpose of curing the same; together with the privilege of hunting, gathering roots and berries, and pasturing their horses on all open and unclaimed lands. Provided, however, That they shall not take shell-fish from any beds staked or cultivated by citizens; and provided, also, that they shall alter all stallions not intended for breeding, and keep up and confine the stallions themselves.

ARTICLE 4
In consideration of the above cession, the United States agree to pay to the said tribes and bands the sum of twenty-five thousand dollars, in the following manner, that is to say: For the first year after the ratification hereof, two thousand five hundred dollars; for the next two years, two thousand dollars each year; for the next three years, one thousand six hundred dollars each year; for the next four years, one thousand three hundred dollars each year; for the next five years, one thousand dollars each year; and for the next five years, seven hundred dollars each year. All of which sums of money shall be applied to the use and benefit of the said Indians under the directions of the President of the United States, who may from time to time, determine at his discretion upon what beneficial objects to expend the same; and the superintendent of Indian affairs, or other proper officer, shall each year inform the President of the wishes of said Indians in respect thereto.

ARTICLE 5
To enable the said Indians to remove to and settle upon such reservation as may be selected for them by the President, and to clear, fence, and break up a sufficient quantity of land for cultivation, the United States further agree to pay the sum of two thousand five hundred dollars, to be laid out and expended under the direction of the President, and in such manner as he shall approve.

ARTICLE 6
The President may hereafter, when in his opinion the interests of the Territory shall require, and the welfare of the said Indians be promoted by it, remove them from said reservation or reservations to such other suitable place or places within said Territory as he may deem fit, on remunerating them for their improvements and the expenses of their removal, or may consolidate them with other friendly tribes or bands, in which latter case the annuities, payable to the consolidated tribes respectively, shall also be consolidated; and he may further, at his discretion, cause the whole or any portion of the lands to be reserved, or of such other land as may be selected in lieu thereof, to be surveyed into lots, and assign the same to such individuals or families as are willing to avail themselves of the privilege, and will locate on the same as a permanent home, on the same terms and subject to the same regulations as are provided in the sixth article of the treaty with the Omahas, so far as the same may be applicable. Any substantial improvements heretofore made by any Indians, and which they shall be compelled to abandon in consequence of this treaty, shall be valued under the direction of the President, and payment made accordingly therefor.

ARTICLE 7
The annuities of the aforesaid tribes and bands shall not be taken to pay the debts of individuals.

ARTICLE 8
The said tribes and bands acknowledge their dependence on the Government of the United States, and promise to be friendly with all citizens thereof, and pledge themselves to commit no depredations on the property of such citizens; and should any one or more of them violate this pledge, and the fact be satisfactorily proven before the agent, the property taken shall be returned, or in default thereof, or if injured or destroyed, compensation may be made by the Government out of their annuities. Nor will they make war on any other tribe except in self-defence, but will submit all matters of difference between them and other Indians to the Government of the United States, or its agent, for decision and abide thereby; and if any of the said Indians commit any

depredations on any other Indians within the Territory, the same rule shall prevail as is prescribed in this article in case of depredations against citizens. And the said tribes and bands agree not to shelter or conceal offenders against the laws of the United States, but to deliver them to the authorities for trial.

ARTICLE 9
The above tribes and bands are desirous to exclude from their reservations the use of ardent spirits, and to prevent their people from drinking the same, and therefore it is provided that any Indian belonging to said tribes who is guilty of bringing liquor into said reservations, or who drinks liquor, may have his or her proportion of the annuities withheld from him or her, for such time as the President may determine.

ARTICLE 10
The United States further agree to establish at the general agency for the district of Puget Sound, within one year from the ratification hereof, and to support for a period of twenty years, an agricultural and industrial school, to be free to the children of the said tribes and bands in common with those of the other tribes of said district, and to provide the said school with a suitable instructor or instructors, and also to provide a smithy and carpenter's shop, and furnish them with the necessary tools, and to employ a blacksmith, carpenter, and farmer for a term of twenty years, to instruct the Indians in their respective occupations. And the United States further agree to employ a physician to reside at the said central agency, who shall furnish medicine and advice to their sick, and shall vaccinate them; the expenses of the said school, shops, employees, and medical attendance to be defrayed by the United States, and not deducted from their annuities.

ARTICLE 11
The said tribes and bands agree to free all slaves now held by them, and not to purchase or acquire others hereafter.

ARTICLE 12
The said tribes and bands finally agree not to trade at Vancouver's Island or elsewhere out of the dominions of the United States, nor

shall foreign Indians be permitted to reside on their reservations without consent of the superintendent or agent.

ARTICLE 13
This treaty shall be obligatory on the contracting parties as soon as the same shall be ratified by the President and Senate of the United States.

In testimony whereof, the said Isaac I. Stevens, governor and superintendent of Indian affairs, and the undersigned chiefs, headmen, and delegates of the aforesaid tribes and bands of Indians, have hereunto set their hands and seals, at Olympia, January 25, 1856, and on the Qui-nai-elt River, July 1, 1855.

Isaac I. Stevens, Governor and Sup't of Indian Affairs.
Tah-ho-lah, Head Chief Qui-nite-'l tribe, his x mark. (L.S.)
How-yat'l, Head Chief Quil-ley-yute tribe, his x mark. (L.S.)
Kal-lape, Sub-chief Quil-ley-hutes, his x mark. (L.S.)
Tah-ah-ha-wht'l, Sub-chief Quil-ley-hutes, his x mark. (L.S.)
Lay-le-whash-er, his x mark. (L.S.)
E-mah-lah-cup, his x mark. (L.S.)
Ash-chak-a-wick, his x mark. (L.S.)
Ay-a-quan, his x mark. (L.S.)
Yats-see-o-kop, his x mark. (L.S.)
Karts-so-pe-ah, his x mark. (L.S.)
Quat-a-de-tot'l, his x mark. (L.S.)
Now-ah-ism, his x mark. (L.S.)
Cla-kish-ka, his x mark. (L.S.)
Kler-way-sr-hun, his x mark. (L.S.)
Quar-ter-heit'l, his x mark. (L.S.)
Hay-nee-si-oos, his x mark. (L.S.)
Hoo-e-yas'lsee, his x mark. (L.S.)
Quilt-le-se-mah, his x mark. (L.S.)
Qua-lats-kaim, his x mark. (L.S.)
Yah-le-hum, his x mark. (L.S.)
Je-tah-let-shin, his x mark. (L.S.)
Ma-ta-a-ha, his x mark. (L.S.)
Wah-kee-nah, Sub-chief Qui-nite'l tribe, his x mark. (L.S.)
Yer-ay-let'l, Sub-chief, his x mark. (L.S.)
Silley-mark'l, his x mark. (L.S.)

Cher-lark-tin, his x mark. (L.S.)
How-yat-'l, his x mark. (L.S.)
Kne-she-guartsh, Sub-chief, his x mark. (L.S.)
Klay-sumetz, his x mark. (L.S.)
Kape, his x mark. (L.S.)
Hay-et-lite-'l, or John, his x mark. (L.S.)
Executed in the presence of us; the words "or tracts," in the II. article, and "next," in the IV. article, being interlined prior to execution.
M. T. Simmons, special Indian agent.
H. A. Goldsborough, commissary, &c.
B. F. Shaw, interpreter.
James Tilton, surveyor-general WashingtonTerritory.
F. Kennedy.
J. Y. Miller.
H. D. Cock.

Jan. 25, 1856. Ratified Mar. 8, 1859. Proclaimed, Apr. 11, 1859.

Preliminary articles of a treaty of peace and friendship between the United States and the Spokane nation of Indians, 1858

ARTICLE 1
Hostilities shall cease between the United States and the Spokane nation of Indians from and after this date.

ARTICLE 2
The chiefs and headmen of the Spokane Indians, for and in behalf of the whole nation, promise to deliver up to the United States all property in their possession belonging either to the government or to individual white persons.

ARTICLE 3
The chiefs and headmen of the Spokane Indians, for and in behalf of the whole nation, promise and agree to deliver to the officer in command of the United States troops who commenced the attack upon Lieutenant Colonel Steptoe, contrary to the orders of their chiefs, and further to deliver as aforesaid at least one chief and four men with their families as hostages for their future good conduct.

ARTICLE 4
The chiefs and headmen of the Spokane nation of Indians promise, for and in behalf of the whole tribe, that all white persons shall at all times and places pass through their country unmolested, and further, that no Indians hostile to the United States shall be allowed to pass through or remain in their country.

ARTICLE 5
The foregoing conditions being fully complied with by the Spokane nation, the officer in command of the United States troops promises that no war shall be made upon the Spokanes, and further, that the men delivered up, whether as prisoners or hostages, shall in nowise be injured, and shall, within the period of one year, be restored to their nation.

ARTICLE 6
It is agreed by both of the aforesaid parties that this treaty shall also extend to and include the Nez Percés nation of Indians.

Done at the headquarters of the expedition against the northern Indians at camp on the Ned-Whauld (or Lahtoo) Washington Territory, this twenty-third of September, eighteen hundred and fifty-eight.

G. Wright
Colonel 9th Infantry, Commanding United States Troops

Pohlatkin
Spokan Garry
Skul-hull   his x mark
Moist-turm   his x mark
Ski-ki-ah-men   his x mark
She-luh-ki-its-ze   his x mark
Mol-mol-e.muh   his x mark
Ki-ah-mene   his x mark
Hoh-Hoh-mee   his x mark
Huse-tesh-him-high   his x mark
Nul-shil-she-hil-sote his x mark
Che-lah-him-sko   his x mark

Huit-sute-tah	his x mark
Keh-ko	his x mark
Qualt-til-tose-sume or Big Star	
	his x mark
Chey-yal-kote	his x mark
Quoi-quoi-yow	his x mark
In-sko-me-nay	his x mark
Its-che-mon-nee	his x mark
It-tem-mee-koh (son of Pohlatkin)	
	his x mark
Schil-cha-hun	his x mark
Meh-mah-icht-such	his x mark
Be-noit	his x mark
So-yar-ole-kim	his x mark
Se-may-koh-lee	his x mark
Sil-so-tee-chee	his x mark
See-che-nie	his x mark
Ko-lim-chin	his x mark
Ho-ho-mish	his x mark
Ski-ime	his x mark
Se-ra-min-home	his x mark
We-yil-sho	his x mark
Che-nee-yah	his x mark
Sko-moh-it-kan	his x mark
Quoit-quoit-il-nee	his x mark
Ped-daltze	his x mark

Witnesses
E D Keys, Captain 3d Artillery
Wm N Grier, Brevet Major United States Army
J F Hammond, Assistant Surgeon United States Army
R W Kirkham, Captain Assistant Quartermaster
F F Dent, Captain 9th Infantry
Charles S Winder, Captain 9th Infantry
James A Hardie, Captain 3d Artillery
A B Fleming, 1st Lieutenant 9th Infantry
Jno F Randolph, Assistant Surgeon United States Army
R O Tyler, 1 Lieutenant 3d Artillery
H B Lyon, 2d Lieutenant 3d Artillery
Lawrence Kip, 2d Lieutenant 3d Artillery

J Howard, 2d Lieutenant 3d Artillery

Preliminary articles of a treaty of peace and friendship between the United States and the Coeur d' Alene Indians, 1858

ARTICLE 1
Hostilities between the United States and the Coeur d' Alene Indians shall cease from and after this date, September 17, 1858.

ARTICLE 2
The chiefs and headmen of the Coeur d' Alene Indians, for and in behalf of the whole nation, agree and promise to surrender to the United States all property in their possession belonging either to the government or to individuals, whether said property was captured or abandoned by the troops of the United States.

ARTICLE 3
The chiefs and headmen of the Coeur d' Alene nation agree to surrender to the United States the men who commenced the battle with Lieutenant Colonel Steptoe, contrary to orders of their chiefs, and also to give at least one chief and four men, with their families, to the officer in command of the troops as hostages for their future good conduct.

ARTICLE 4
The chiefs and headmen of the Coeur d' Alene nation promise that all white person shall travel through their country unmolested, and that no Indian hostile to the United States shall be allowed within the limits of their country.

ARTICLE 5
The officer in command of the United States troops, for and in behalf of the government, promises that if the foregoing conditions are fully complied with no war shall be made upon the Coeur d' Alene nation; and further, that the men who are to be surrendered, whether those who commenced the fight with Lieutenant Colonel Steptoe or as hostages for the future good conduct of the Coeur d' Alene nation, shall in nowise be injured, and shall, within one year from the date herefore, be restored to their nations.

ARTICLE 6
It is agreed by both of the aforesaid contraction parties that when the foregoing articles shall have been fully complied with, a permanent treaty of peace and friendship shall be made.

ARTICLE 7
It is agreed by the chiefs and headmen of the Coeur d' Alene nation that this treaty of peace and friendship shall extend also to include the Nez Percés nation of Indians.

Done at the headquarters of the expedition against northern Indians, at the Coeur d' Alene mission, Washington Territory, this 17th day of September, 1858.

G Wright
Colonel 9th Infantry, commanding

Mil-kap-si	his x mark
Sal-tize	his x mark
Vincent	his x mark
Joseph	his x mark
Jean Pierre	his x mark
Pierre Pauline	his x mark
Louis Margeni	his x mark
Cypronani	his x mark
Augustin	his x mark
Paul	his x mark
Bonaventure	his x mark
Cassimere	his x mark
Bernard	his x mark
Anthony	his x mark
Leo	his x mark
Patricia	his x mark
Pierre	his x mark
Jean Pierre	his x mark

Witnesses
E D Keys, Captain 3d Artillery
W N Grier, Brevet Major United States Army
R W Kirkham, Captain and Assistant Quartermaster

F F Dent, Captain 9th Infantry
C S Winder, Captain 9th Infantry
J F Hammond, Assistant Surgeon United States Army
Jas A Hardie, Captain 3d Artillery
H G Gibson, 1st Lieutenant 3d Artillery
R O Tyler, 1st Lieutenant 3d Artillery
Jno F Randolph, Assistant Surgeon United States Army
H B Davidson, 1st Lieutenant 1st Dragoons
W D Pender, 2nd Lieutenant 1st Dragoons

Letters: Apprehensions towards war
Letter from Fr. Charles Pandosy to Fr. Toussaint Mesplie, April 1853[76]

I start in two days for the mission of Coeur d' Alene. If by the favor of God, I should return alive, I will endeavor to answer the question of the Major [Benjamin Alvord] concerning the manner and customs of Indians, etc.

You ask the reason of my expression, 'if I return alive.' Alas! For I commence my journey in dangerous times. Yes, the clouds are gathering upon all hands, the winds begin to lower the tempest is pent up ready to burst. From your silence I know not what to think- truly I know not what to think. You are upon the spot which will be the first victim of this tempest, and you say not a word. I will say, in the words of him who arraigned Cataline and his accomplices, "The Senate sees these things. The Senate sees thes things, and remains immovable spectators.' But perhaps you are not aware of the plot which is being laid. Yes, if the reports which reach me are true, there is among the savages a second Cataline, another Ingurtha, on of the descendants of Machiaveli. Yes, a real Machiaveli menaces Oregon! If these reports are true, it is well that you take warning, and make them known to the Major. But I will beg that he who gives the alarm, as well as the place whence it comes, may remain unknown, for reasons which you will appreciate. For if the Indians know whence comes the alarm, there will never be any safety for us in their country, (and nothing

---

[76] Kowrach, *Charles Pandosy*, 75

more can be done for their religious welfare. Our poor converted Indians would become the most unhappy of men, for the rage of their tribes would fall upon their heads. I stop in order to give you the facts.)

The following are the reports which arrive from the Nez Perce country:

A chief of the Upper Nez Perce has killed 30 head of cattle at a feast given to the nation; and this number of animals not being sufficient, seven more were killed. This feast was given in order to unite the hearts of all the Indians together, to make declarations of war against the Americans. Through the who course of the winter I have heard the same thing—that the Cayuse and the Nez Perces have united themselves for war. During the course of last spring I was in the Cayuse country, after they had given a similar feast. I said nothing, because I thought they had a sub-agent who would speak. I said, too, the Indians are like puppies that bark afar off; now, however, hearing what I do, I say the puppy has grown to a full-grown mastiff. I will recount to you what they say. All the Indians on the left bank of the Columbia, from the Blackfeet to the Chinook, inclusive, are t o assemble at the Cayuse country. All on the right bank, through the same extent of country, are to assemble on the Simcoe (or the Yakima) including from Nesqually and its vicinity. The cause of war is, that the Americans are going to seize their lands. Every time that I have heard this project mentioned I have strongly represented its folly. The words were thrown away, cast into the air, for it was represented that the Cayuse and Nez Perces had an understanding, and were united in this matter.

If you wish to know what I have think of this gigantic scheme, I will tell you freely. I don't think all the tribes can be united as one body. I have never known such a union. Besides, those of the Nesqually, can't move so far, having no means of transportation. They are not accustomed to move in this direction, and they are enemies to the P-shwan-wapans, etc., etc. Also, it is impossible for the Indians to unite without the report of its spreading far and wide. How can they unite in such a matter without the noise of reaching you. For, thus far our Indians remain quiet and remain so to this moment. They are alarmed by the rumors they hear; they do not themselves love war. There remains, then in a state of hostility those on the left bank of the Columbia—that is to say, the Cayuse and their adherents in the vicinity of the Umatilla, the Walla Wallas, the Des Chutes, those at the Taie, on the one side: on the other, the Palouse, the Nez Perces and the Snakes. Don't think that I would pass off for saints the Indians in my vicinity; I only say what I think of the reports. I'd not wish them to pass off for better than they are. It is possible that they are in the plot, but I know nothing of it. I know nothing of it from what I see and hear. Now, nothing which has occurred here gives me reason to believe in this plot—in this union of tribes as one man. Nevertheless, I ought to add that Shawawai, one of the small chiefs in our neighborhood, has given away some horses to a great number of Indians, with what object I know not; but it has the appearance of raising followers to go and revenge on the Blackfeet the death of some of their people killed by the latter.

Among the chiefs of the Nez Perces, some wish to make no distinction between Canadians and Americans, but would kill all the Whites in their country, without distinction, trappers or traders. Others wish to preserve the people of the Hudson's Bay Company, because (they say) the are our people, they marry our daughters. Their children are half-Canadian, half our country; we should slay a part of ourselves. What language they hold concerns us, I know not.

But my prolixity wearies you. Perhaps you will think that I am the Livy and you the Tacitus. For in your letter you have never been so short and so concise for the four years I have had the honor of knowing you. Nevertheless, this is the first time I have heard from you this winter, although I have written you often.

Adieu, my dear sir…

Letter from Maj. Gabriel Rains to the Department of the Pacific
January 29, 1854[77]

The time has arrived when it becomes necessary to determine the question of peace or war between the citizens of the United States and Indian tribes on this frontier, east of the "Cascades" and west of the Rocky Mountains…

Indian complaints have been often brought from time to time that white men are locating on their land, against their will,

---

[77] Shannon, *Boise Massacre*, 44-45

and that without respect to their individual possessions, or property, or priority of Indian claimants.

Such statements have been met by informing them that by an act of Congress of the United States, establishing the territorial government of Oregon, (approved, 14 March 1848) "no rights of persons or property now pertaining to the Indians in this country shall be impaired, so long as such rights shall remain unextinguished by treaty between them and the United States."

They also complain of lawless violence, injury, and murder by white men who come among them, some for secret purposes of illegal traffic in spirituous liquors, irresponsible to their laws, and who are uncontrollable by civil law of the Territory of Oregon, which intends "good faith," with inability to carry it out, by barring Indian testimony against them "in any court or in any case whatever."...Under the laws of Oregon these people ordinarily can have no legal prosecutor, nor grand jury legally to represent their cause, and must forever be deprived of justice as long as the disparity in numbers is so great, or a white accomplice chooses to cloak crime...

The Indian tribes immediately concerned are the "Des Chutes" and the "Waseves," some 700 or 800 souls; the "Nez Perces," numbering about 2,500; the "Cayuses" and adjuncts, about 300; the "Snakes," composed of the Bannack, the Shoshones, and Root Diggers, say 3,000; the Shastas, the Unatillas, the Tic, and some others number unknown, say in all about 1,300 warriors.

If any country in the world has ever merited the title of "Indian country" this is it; and yet by legislative enactment this has been erected into Wasco county of Oregon Territory, the largest county ever known, and civil officers appointed where there are but few white citizens, some thirty-five perhaps in all, who claim their right to locate their "donations" where they please (and often irrespective of Indian rights) by an act of Congress making donations to settlers in the Territory of Oregon…This, with a decision of the Supreme Court, sets aside the intercourse law, and bars our right to purge the land of incendiaries who set themselves down among the Indians to commit all crimes with impunity, even murder, with only Indian testimony against them to bring them to justice, which is not available in law.

Many of the squatters are good citizens, but this in not the case with all, far from it, and my predecessor (Major Alvord) having made representations, also the superintendent of Indian affairs, who business mainly it is, having previously done the same, I have been slow been slow to move in the matter until "forbearance ceases to be a virtue" and prompt action is required, doing justice to all, to prevent an Indian war with the Indians tribes combined, between the Cascade and Rocky Mountains.

Though these Indians are very uneasy, yet there is no immediate cause for alarm; still the necessity for prompt action exists…similar to those which gave rise to the Rogue river war. Life for life is the Indian rule, and soon some innocent persons among the whites may suffer for the acts of the guilty,

Within a, short period there have been five men killed, viz.; two by Indians of their own people- cause: spirituous liquor introduced clandestinely, (though Judge Olney, of Oregon, is said to have stated in open court that there is no law to restrain such sales, and the legislature is now making one.) One, a Frenchman, name unknown, in about thirty miles distance, murdered by an Indian. One, an Indian, murdered by a white many, whom I had in confinement to be turned over to civil power, to be released at the Cascades on account of some informality in the action of the magistrate committing, as informed. And still a recent case of another Indian killed by a white man, whom we have now in prison in the guardhouse, and who surrendered himself probably for protection from the infuriated tribe which followed him to this post.

The Indians have been pacified by being promised justice in every case, which I regret to say has not, been accomplished; which state of things under legislative enactments we cannot alter, and which are the citizens themselves, as soon as their civil officers, are properly qualified, with an eye to their own safety, will find it equally impossible under the law, or without further legislation.

The object of this communication is to awaken attention to the state of things on this frontier; to find a way) with the approbation of my superiors) before the Committee on Indian Affairs in Congress, for them in their wisdom, to devise some means of retributive justice in this country of Indians, and among other tribes concerned, securing to each the land on which his lodge stands, and the soil which his squaw cultivates, and defining the rights of the white settler for his better security.

Never a cent has been known to be appropriated for the benefit or improvement of these tribes, yet they are peaceably disposed, if undisturbed.

We are deficient at this post in our proper number of soldiers to fill up the two companies, 106 men, and a company of mounted men is much required…

G J Rains

Major 4th Infantry, commanding post and troops on this frontier

Extract from Fr. Charles Pandosy to Bishop Charles Joseph Eugene de Mazenod
June 5, 1854[78]

Advice given to Chief Kamiakin

It is as I feared, the Whites will take your country as they have taken other countries from the Indians. I came from the land of the White man to the East where the people are thicker than the grass on the hills. Where there are only a few here now, others will come with each year until your country will be overrun with them…You and your lands will be seized and your people driven from their homes. It has been so with other tribes; it will be so with you. You may fight and delay fro a time this invasion, but you cannot avert it. I have lived many summers with you and baptized

---

[78] Kowrach, *Charles Pandosy,* 78

a great may of your people into the faith. I have learned to love you. I cannot advise you or help you. I wish I could.

Letter from the Yakama tribe to the soldiers of the United States, transcribed by Fr. Charles Pandosy[79]
October 7, 1855

Write to the soldiers and tell them we are quiet, friends to the Americans, that we were not thinking of war at all, but the manner in which the governor has talked to us among the Cayuses has irritated us and made us decide that a general war will not end except with the complete extermination of all savages or all Americans.

If the Governor had said to us, my children, I am asking you a parcel of land in each tribe for the Americans, but the land and your country is always yours, we would then have given with good will what he would have asked us and we would have lived with you all as brothers. But he has taken us in small groups and thrown us out of our native country, into a strange land among a people who is our enemy (for between us we are enemies) in a place where our people do not even have enough to eat for themselves.

Then we said, now we know perfectly the heart of the Americans. For a long time, they hanged us without knowing if we are right or wrong, but they have never killed or hanged on American, though there is no place where Americans have not

---

[79] Ibid., 95-97

killed Indians. We are therefore as dogs. They tell us our ancestors had no horses nor cattle, nor corn nor seeds nor instruments to garden, that we have received all of these riches from the Americans; that the country was already full of us and at the same time the Americans chased us from our native land, as if the Americans would tell us: 'We have sent you all things so you could multiply them until my people arrive.' You Americans want, therefore, to make us die of famine little by little. It is better for us to die at one blow. It is you, Governor, who has wanted war, by these words: 'The country will be ours—all tribes, all nations, and all you will go to a designated place and leave your land.'

Our heart was torn when you pronounced these words. You have fired the first shot. Our heart is broken. There is only one breath left in us; we did not have the strength to answer. Then we took common cause with our enemies to defend all together our nationality and our country.

However the war was not going to start so soon, but the Americans who were going to the mines have fired on some Indians because they did not want to give them their women and we have taken the measure to defend ourselves.

After that came Mr. Bolon, who strongly insulted us, threatened us with death when announcing to us that he was going back to the Dalles, from where he would send soldiers to destroy us. Nevertheless, we had let him pass quietly, but after having thought of what he had just told us we went to join him. We were without arms and without any idea to kill him but as he went on talking to us with much harshness and threatened us with soldiers, we have seized him and we have killed him, so that we can say, it is not we who have started war, but we have only defended ourselves.

If the soldiers and American after reading this letter and learning about the motives which bring us to fight, want to retire and treat us in a friendly way, we will consent to put down our arms and to grant them a parcel of land from each different tribe, as long as they do not force us to be exiled from our native country. Otherwise, we are resolved to be cut down and if we lose the men who keep the camp in which are the wives and our children we will kill them rather than see them fall into the hands of the Americans to make them their playthings. For we have hearts and self-respect.

Write this Father Pandosy, to the soldiers and the American so that they can give you an answer and let us know what they think. If they do not answer, it is because they want war; we are at this moment 1,050 men assembled. Some only will go to battle, but as soon as the war is begun the news will spread among all our nations and in a few days we will be more than 10,000. If peace is wanted, we will consent to it, but it must be written to us so we may know about it.

PHOTOS OF HISTORICAL SIGHTS[80]

Andrew Bolon
Klickitat County

Fort Colvile (HBC)
Stevens County

Fort Dalles
Wasco County

Connell's Prairie
Pierce County

---

[80] All photos are from the author

Colville-Walla Walla Road
Spokane County

Fort Simcoe (USA)
Yakima County

Spokane House
Spokane County

Camp Washington
Spokane County

Fort Vancouver (HBC)
Clark County

Point Elliot Treaty
Snohomish County

Port Gamble Cemetery
Kitsap County

Mission of the Sacred Heart
Kootenai County

Fort Nez Perces (HBC)
Walla Walla County

Walla Walla Council Grounds
Walla Walla County

Plante's Ferry
Spokane County

Fort Maloney
Pierce County

Saint Joseph's Mission
Yakima County

Battle of Tohotomine
Whitman County

Battle of Spokane Plains
Spokane County

Medicine Creek Treaty
Thurston County

Fort Colville (USA)
Stevens County

Horse Slaughter site
Spokane County

Battle of Frenchtown & St. Rose
Mission
Walla Walla County

Tshimakain Mission Site
Stevens County

Bibliography

Adams, George, *General William S. Harney: Prince of Dragoons,* (Lincoln, NE: University of Nebraska Press, 2001)

Ambrose, Stephen, *Undaunted Courage* ,(New York: Touchstone, 1997)

Becher, Edmund, *History, Government and Resources of the Spokane area,* (Spokane, WA: Spokane Community College Print Shop, 1965)

Bird, Anne, *Boise, the peaceful valley,* (Caldwell, ID: The Caxton Printers, 1934)

Bischoff, William, SJ, *We were not summer soldiers: The Indian war diary of Plympton J. Kelly 1855-1856,* (Tacoma, WA: Washington State Historical Society, 1976)

Breshears, Guy, *Major Granville Haller: Dismissed with Malice,* (Bowie, MD: Heritage Books, 2006)

Burns, Robert, SJ, *The Jesuits and the Indian Wars of the Northwest,* (New Haven: Yale University Press, 1966)

Cebula, Larry, "Religious Change and Plateau Indians: 1500-1850" (Ph.D. diss, College of William and Mary, 1999.)

Chamberlain, Martin N, *Granville Haller: Leader,* (Victoria, BC: Trafford, 2005)

Cummings, Al, *San Juan: The Powder-keg Island,* (Friday Harbor, WA: Beach Combers, Inc., 1987)

Frazer, Robert, *Forts of the West, Military Forts and Presidios and Posts commonly called forts west of the Mississippi River to 1898,* (Norman, OK: University of Oklahoma Press, 1972)

Gilbert, Frank, *Historical Sketches of Walla Walla, Whitman, Columbia and Garfield Counties, Washington Territory,* (Portland, OR: Printing and Lithographing House of A.G. Walling)

Grant, Frederic James, *History of Seattle Washington with illustrations and biographical sketches of some of its prominent men and pioneers.* (New York: American Publishing and Engraving, 1891)

Guie, H. Dean, *Bugles in the Valley: Garnett's Fort Simcoe,* (Portland: Oregon Historical Society, 1977)

Haller family letters, transcribed by Martin N. Chamberlain, 1853-59. Island County [WA] Historical Society

Haller, Granville, "San Juan and Secession" (paper presented at the meeting of the Loyal Legion, Seattle, WA, 16 Jan. 1896), Special Collections, Eastern Washington University, Cheney, WA.

-----, *The Dismissal of Major Granville O. Haller of the Regular Army of the United States by order of the Secretary of War in Special Orders, No. 331, of July 25th, 1863* (Paterson, NJ: The Daily Guardian Office, 1863)

Haller, Theodore, "Life and Public Services of Colonel Granville O. Haller, Soldier, Citizen and Pioneer," *The Washington Historian,* Vol. 1, No. 3 (April 1900), 102-109

Hemphill, John, *West Pointers and Early Washington: The Contribution of U.S. Military Academy Graduates to the Development of the Washington Territory, from the Oregon Trail to the Civil War 1834-1862* (Seattle: The West Point Society of Puget Sound, Inc., 1992)

Kirk, Ruth and Alexander, Carmela, *Exploring Washington's Past: A road guide to history,* (Seattle, WA: University of Washington Press, 1990)

Knuth, Priscilla, *"Picturesque" Frontier: The Army's Fort Dalles,* (Portland: Oregon Historical Society Press, 1987)

Kowrach, Edward J., *Mie. Charles Pandosy, O.M.I.: A Missionary of the Northwest,* (Fairfield, WA: Ye Galleon Press, 1992)

Manring, Benjamin, *Conquest of the Coeur d' Alenes, Spokanes & Palouses,* (Fairfield, WA: Ye Galleon Press, 1975)

McWhorter, Lucullus, *Tragedy of the Wahk-Shum: The death of Andrew J. Bolon, Yakima Indian Agent as told by Su-el-lil, Eyewitness,* (Issaquah WA, Great Eagle Publishing, Inc., 1994)

Miller, Christopher, *Prophetic Worlds: Indians and Whites on the Columbia Plateau,* (Seattle, University of Washington Press, 2003)

Morgan, Murray, *Puget's Sound, A narrative of early Tacoma and the southern sound,* (Seattle, WA: University of Washington Press, 1979)

Murray, Keith, *The Pig War,* (Tacoma, WA: Washington State Historical Society, 1968)

Nelson, Kurt, *Fighting for Paradise: A Military history of the Pacific Northwest,* (Yardley, PA: Westholme Publishing, LLC, 2007)

Prucha, Francis *A guide to the military posts of the United States, 1789-1895,* (Madison, WI: The State Historical Society of Wisconsin, 1964)

Scheuerman, Richard and Finley, Michael, *Finding Chief Kamiakin: The Life and Legacy of a Northwest Patriot,* (Pullman, WA: Washington State University Press, 2008)

Schlicke, Carl, *General George Wright: Guardian of the Pacific Coast,* (Norman, OK: University of Oklahoma Press, 1988)

-----, "Long Road to Vindication for Accused Northwest Soldier," *Columbia,* Vol. 1, No. 1 (Summer 1988), 21-29

Settle, Raymond, ed., *The March of the Mounted Riflemen: First United States Military Expedition to travel the full length of the Oregon Trail from Fort Leavenworth to Fort Vancouver May to October, 1849 as recorded in the journals of Major Osborne Cross and George Gibbs and the official report of Colonel Lorning,* (Lincoln, NE: University of Nebraska, 1989)

Shannon, Donald H., *The Boise Massacre of the Oregon Trail,* (Caldwell, ID: Snake Country Publishing, 2004)

The Avalon Project at Yale Law School, Thomas Jefferson's First Inaugural Address,
http://www.yale.edu/laweb/avalon/presiden/inaug/jefinau1.htm
(accessed 16 October 2004)

-----, Inaugural Address of James Knox Polk,
http://www.yale.edu/laweb/avalon/presiden/inaug/polk.htm (accessed 16 October 2004)

Trafzer, Clifford E. & Scheuerman, Richard D., *Renegade Tribe: The Palouse Indians and the Invasion of the Inland Pacific Northwest,* (Pullman, WA: Washington State University Press, 1986)

US Congress, *Annual Message from the President of the United States to the two Houses of Congress, Department of the Pacific, 1855,* 34th Congress, 1st session, 1855, House Ex. Doc. No. 1, Part 2, Serial 811

-----, *Annual Message from the President of the United States to the two Houses of Congress, Report of the Secretary of War, 1856*, 34th Congress, 3rd session, S. Exec. Doc. 5, Pt. 2, Serial 876

-----, *Annual Message from the President of the United States to the two Houses of Congress, Department of the Pacific, 1858*, 35th Congress, 2nd session, House Ex. Doc. 2, Vol. 2, Pt. 2, Serial 998

Utley, Robert, *Frontiersmen in Blue: The United States Army and the Indian, 1848-1865*, (Lincoln, NE: University of Nebraska Press, 1981)

Vouri, Michael, *The Pig War: Standoff at Griffin Bay*, (Friday Harbor, WA: Griffin Bay Bookstore, 1999)

Whitman, Narcissa, *The letters of Narcissa Whitman, 1836-1847*, (Fairfield, WA: Ye Galleon Press, 1996)

Young, Ronald, O.M.I., "The Mission of the Missionary Oblates of Mary Immaculate to the Oregon Territory (1847-1860)" (Ph.D. diss., Pontifica Universitas Gregoriana, Romae, 2000.)

ABOUT THE AUTHOR

Guy Breshears was born in Spokane, Washington and has always been interested in the Indian wars around the region. He received his BAE in Social Science Education and MA in History from Eastern Washington University in Cheney, Washington. With an interest in the advancement of knowledge, understanding and preservation of the military events that took place in the territory he has lectured to teachers and university students. Finally, he successfully petitioned the Washington State Department of Transportation to erect Heritage Marker signs in Four Lakes, Washington showing the direction to the Battle of Four Lakes marker. He currently resides in Hong Kong.

www.ingramcontent.com/pod-product-compliance
Lightning Source LLC
Chambersburg PA
CBHW060818190426
43197CB00038B/2000